Standing up for Education

Edited by
Louise Regan and Tom Unterrainer

Christine Blower
Siobhan Collingwood
Mary Compton
Jeremy Corbyn MP
Kevin Courtney
Polly Donnison
Alan Gibbons
Rosie Hancock
Jill Huish
Julie James
Sam Keely
Gawain Little
Kristine Mayle
Philip Moriarty
Tony Simpson
Kiri Tunks
Nadia Whittome

SPOKESMAN
Nottingham

First published in 2016

Spokesman
Russell House, Bulwell Lane,
Nottingham, NG6 0BT, England
www.spokesmanbooks.com

ISBN 978 085124 858 5

A cataloguing-in-publication (CIP) record is available from the British Library

Printed and bound in Nottingham by Russell Press Ltd
www.russellpress.com 0115 9784505

Contents

Introduction

Louise Regan and Tom Unterrainer

This collection of essays and articles has been produced by teachers, parents, trade unionists and students. Its purpose is to address the deep and growing crisis in our schools, to document the dimensions of this crisis, and to point towards potential solutions. This book is intended as fuel for all those who have been involved in *Stand Up for Education* and other campaigns. We hope that it will help to grow and sustain such campaigns. We also hope that the contents will be considered by those people in Labour and other political parties involved in formulating and renewing education policies.

The contributors present their own views and ideas. Whilst there is no uniformity of approach, no single 'line' that we all follow, the contributors are united in their agreement with Jeremy Corbyn's assertion that 'education is a fundamental right'. As obvious as this assertion may seem to readers, it is in fact a vigorously contested notion, as are concepts of what a 'good education' actually looks like. Nowhere is this more obvious than in schools themselves.

The term 'crisis' is over used and has become a cliché to many ears, but its use cannot be avoided. How else to describe the complete lack of confidence expressed by the teaching profession and a growing number of parents in the political 'leadership' of the Cameron Government? How else to characterise the manifold issues that weigh on teachers, parents and – most importantly – the young people and children in our schools? In what other way are we supposed to conceive of a government that refused either to address these problems or take responsibility for them? Will the new Prime Minister, Theresa May, and her Secretary of State for Education, Justine Greening, take responsibility for the crisis and do something about it?

It is impossible to say in advance whether the new government will take a different course to that dictated by the favoured policies of Michael Gove and Nicky Morgan. What we can say is that such a change of course would represent a significant break with the dominant trends in education policy accepted by a succession of British governments. Such a change would also go against the grain of the global movement for education 'reform'. These policies are important with regards to Justine Greening who, during her tenure at the Department for International Development, worked with private education companies to deliver educational 'aid' to the developing world. Also of importance is Theresa May's longstanding sympathy for 'grammar schools' and, by implication, a two-tier, selective education system. Whatever the differences and departures with previous policy agendas, whatever the nuances or adjustments, there is much work to do if we are to create an education system fit purpose, fit for the children and young people in our schools.

If *Standing up for Education* inspires just one additional teacher to become an activist for a better education system, then it will have served its purpose. If this book encourages just one parent to start a community campaign for a better education system, it will have done its job. If this book prompts just one student to organise and represent their interests within the education system, it will have done its job. As all teachers know, books can be a powerful force in society. We hope this one will make some difference.

1

Education is a fundamental right

Jeremy Corbyn MP

On 25 March 2016, Jeremy Corbyn became the first leader of the Labour Party to address the annual conference of the National Union of Teachers. Following years in which the views and opinions of teachers were ignored by politicians of all persuasions, Jeremy's intervention represents much more than a symbolic first. What follows is a transcript of his speech.

I think history proves me correct that I am the first ever Labour leader to speak to a National Union of Teachers conference. I do that because I'm very proud to call myself a trade unionist. I've been a trade union member all my life and I will be until the day I die. I'm proud to be in a party that is campaigning against the Trade Union Bill: the Bill, if it becomes an Act … [will be repealed] in 2020. Because strengthening trade union and employment rights – fundamental human rights – strengthens our society. I want you to know that we will stand up for trade union rights in every profession, every area, and I absolutely admire and value the work of the trade unions in the teaching profession, and the National Union of Teachers. We will be standing alongside you, not just for teachers, but for all education staff, teaching assistants, and ancillary staff, because it's a team that makes a school work, it's a team that provides the support and comforts that our children need in schools, and I understand that very well.

Why do I understand it so well? Because my late mother was a maths teacher and a member of the National Union of Teachers. And as a maths teacher she would be much in demand now, because I'm very well aware of the shortages. There are one or two pupils around the country that need extra tuition: one of them is George Osborne. Having just presented to Parliament a budget that simply doesn't add up – in fact it has a massive great black hole in it – I think maybe a little extra tuition would be helpful to him. Is anybody offering? Somebody, come on, please!

But it's also a very strange budget because it suddenly headed off in the direction of education structures, and then said there was going to be forced academisation of all schools. Now let's be clear, this is an ideological attack on teachers and local parental accountability: it was nowhere in any Tory manifesto, it's something that's just been dreamt up at the last minute and stuck into the budget. I want schools to be accountable to their parents and their communities, not as a process of asset-stripping education facilities to be handed over to somebody else. So the first thing that's always done ahead of privatisation of any services is to attack the skilled staff, so it's about breaking national pay bargaining, expanding the use of unqualified teachers, driving down pay, driving down terms and conditions, and driving down standards.

There is not a shred of evidence that academies automatically improve standards. There are very real fears about the intentions of this government and those who pay themselves exorbitant salaries to run academy chains. Now, I don't suppose there's too much love in this hall for Sir Michael Wilshaw, but he recently reported to the Education Secretary that focused inspections in seven of the largest academy chains showed a lack of improvement and in some cases a decline in standards – quite important observations. Lucy Powell, our Education shadow spokesperson, spoke at your rally in London on Wednesday night [23 March 2016], to assure you that Labour will be fiercely opposing those plans. And we will. 80 per cent of community primary schools are rated 'good' or 'outstanding'. Taking away local control and accountability is actually just demonstrating how hollow the Tories' policies on this area of devolution are. Cutting out local authorities will mean councils no longer have the power to ensure sufficient school places in their areas.

There is a crisis in our schools now. Children are facing rising class sizes; there is a shortage of teachers; and parents already face a crisis, in some places, in school places. Forced academisation will do nothing to address any of those problems, yet in Osborne's budget over £600 million has been allocated to a needless reorganisation that has addressed not a single issue that matters to teachers, parents, or pupils. So you see where the priorities are: spending money on a reorganisation nobody wants, to reduce the influence and control of local authorities, in order to bring in unaccountable academies. Those are the Tory priorities; they are absolutely not ours. So they asset-strip and cut school funding – in real terms. Their values are absolutely wrong.

Government policies impact in many ways on children, and as teachers you deal every day with the emotional and stress problems that many children face all over the country. The upheavals in their lives, caused by a housing crisis, caused by having to move very frequently because of high levels of private sector rent, and issues like that – you as teachers deal with those problems day in, day out. You feel the stress our children face because of inadequate housing policies in this country, you feel the stress of child poverty; housing costs up and half a million children living in poverty in this country, and over a million families using food banks. There is something very sad when parents ought to be delighted at the prospect of a school holiday, to spend time with their children, possibly to go away; for some families, a school holiday is a total nightmare. No longer will the children get breakfast in school, no longer will they get lunch in school, those children are going to have a very hard time because of the poverty of their families. Not right, not good, not necessary in modern Britain. We can, and should, do things differently.

It's small wonder that the attainment gap is now wider than when David Cameron became Prime Minister. Disadvantaged children are getting left further and further behind. Social deprivation is holding back thousands of children, children simply unable to concentrate properly because they arrive at school too hungry to be able to learn properly. I know of so many of your members in so many schools who reach into their own pockets to give children something to eat in order to start the day. I admire you for doing it, but you shouldn't have to do it. And so, in Wales, Labour has acted, bringing in free school breakfasts for all primary schools, and despite the block grant being cut by over a billion pounds from central government, the Welsh Labour government has maintained the meal system and the free breakfast system. I think they should be applauded for that – well done them on having their priorities right. Children are stressed by their parents' financial worries, caused by job and benefit insecurity, and insecurity in housing. Homelessness has risen every year this government has been in office. Child poverty is forecast to rise every year throughout this parliament. This is the fundamental issue.

Instead of constructing a market in the education system, the government should be alleviating the obstacles that hold back our children. A decent government would also know that the best advice on improving education comes from teachers. So they should listen to you and alleviate the problems you face. The pressure of work forced more teachers to quit last year than ever – 50,000 – and the government has now missed its teacher training recruitment targets for the last four years. This has resulted, as you well know, in half a million children now being taught in classes over 31 in primary schools. One in four schools increase their use of supply teachers; one in six use non-specialists to cover vacancies; and more than one in ten are resorting to using unqualified staff to teach lessons. Labour wants to work with you, with parents, with pupils, with local authorities, with our communities, to defend education – the principle of education – and stop these plans of forced 'academisation'.

To me, education is a fundamental right for all of us. Those who fought and campaigned for free state education in the nineteenth century, those who campaigned more and more for raising the school leaving age, and all the other things that we've campaigned for. Those who campaigned for free adult education … [did it] so that everybody, wherever they come from, whatever their background, whatever their abilities, can make the most of their lives, can have access to the wonderful body of learning that should be available for everybody. Surely that is the principle on which we should approach education policy, not the marketisation and academisation of our education system.

I want to say thank you to this union for the work it has done. I want to say, also, a special and personal thank you to Christine Blower. She's standing down as General Secretary in May 2016. She took over at a very difficult time, after the death of Steve Sinnott, and she steered this campaign with vigour and principles, and it's been a pleasure to be with her at so many events, conferences, and demonstrations over the years. I'm sure you'll all appreciate, as the rest of us do, the huge work that Christine has done. Christine, thank you so much. I know she's going to play a huge role in your union, in the Labour movement, in all the great campaigns that we're all involved with, because when we do things together, when we campaign together, when we work together, when we have that dream and that vision of a decent society where everybody can participate and everybody can achieve, and we don't have to have the grotesque levels of poverty and inequality in our society, we're a much more effective, much more efficient, much happier society. Thank you very much for inviting me here today.

Transcribed by Nicole Morris

2

The progressive purpose of education

Keeping the idea alive

Christine Blower

In the early 1970s the world and education were very different from what we see and experience today. Joining the staff at Holland Park School, having been centrally recruited by the Inner London Education Authority (ILEA) as a bright-eyed, enthusiastic and probably woefully underprepared probationer, was as scary as it was exciting. There was a clear sense in those days that, whatever and wherever it may have been in earlier decades, the National Union of Teachers (NUT) was undoubtedly the progressive voice of teachers. The NUT was concerned not just with pay (we still had negotiating rights through the Burnham Committee) but also about curriculum and rights issues.

Joining the NUT – or rather continuing in membership from having been a student member – was an obvious choice. If you taught in London, indeed in most of England and Wales, the NUT was the only union to join. The prominence of the Inner London Teachers' Association (ILTA) would have made any other choice all but absurd.

It seems unreal now that in the early seventies there was no National Curriculum. Strictly speaking, Religious Education was the only subject which was mandated. At Holland Park only English was compulsory in the 4th and 5th year, although it was joined by maths in the later years of the decade. Inspection meant a visit from one of 'Her Majesty's Inspectors' maybe once or twice in a career and then the reports remained the property of the school and the Local Education Authority (LEA). The pay system was national, in place in every school with a staffing establishment set by the Local Education Authority for every school, and an LEA which could determine how many school places were necessary and build and open (or sometimes close) schools according to need.

Even in those days workload was an issue, but the essential difference was the locus of control. Many teachers worked many an evening and weekends developing exams and schemes of work. They did it, however, on a voluntary basis and because they believed in what they were doing. The long hours were entirely self-directed and, frankly, often invigorating.

There were, of course, many problems in the 1970s, too. Society was more racist, more sexist, and certainly more homophobic. There was a real concern in some authorities to make sure that black children, perhaps in particular black boys, were not let down by the schooling system. There was much good and some rather poor anti-racist training for teachers, and a lot of activity from self-organised groups such as 'All London Teachers Against Racism and Fascism'. The ILEA, despite some faults, was a progressive authority which, of course, ultimately made it a target for the Tories to abolish.

Fast forward to 2016 and we see a very different educational landscape: an imposed National Curriculum with associated testing of incredibly burdensome and stressful proportions; the Office for Standards in Education (Ofsted); deregulation of pay; and a plan to demolish what remains of the locally accountable education system we once enjoyed. Many who count amongst our numbers in the Union now will have spent their own entire education in the system of National Curriculum and associated testing. As teachers they will only have worked in that system. It is clear from the reaction of primary members of the NUT to the 2016 tests that the system has to change.

Along the way there have been many changes of policy at national level from various governments. Most, although not all, have been in some way opposed by the NUT. It's interesting to recall that more authorities went comprehensive under Margaret Thatcher than any other Secretary of State for Education, but that is just an accident of timing. For a serious consideration of policy shifts from 1944 to the present, Ken Jones' book, *Education in Britain*, is an invaluable resource.

From Local Financial Management, trialled in Cambridgeshire, to Local Management of Schools, from Grant Maintained Status to the creation of Academies, initially under Tony Blair, there have been fears for the future of the education system more widely and the NUT in particular. But the NUT has survived and thrived. The attacks on the trade union movement in the Trade Union Act of 2016 raise serious questions about how the Union will organise going forward, but organise it will. There is strength and depth in the structure and membership of the National Union of Teachers and an orientation towards activism on behalf not just of members' pay conditions but also of an education system which, in the well-worn expression used by Education International, is a 'human and civil right and a public good and of course of high quality'.

Where once there was probably something of a consensus on what is meant by 'quality', this is now contended. In this context the role of the National Union of Teachers is to provide a vision for what education could and should be. In recent years, the Union has fought to keep progressive ideas about the purpose of education on the agenda. It has been an uphill struggle, faced with governments who have swallowed the 'Global Education Reform Movement' (GERM) agenda hook, line and sinker. Arguments for alternatives to GERM are usually built on an examination of education in successful jurisdictions elsewhere in the world: Finland being an example of an anti-GERM success, and Sweden an example of the opposite. Sweden has fallen spectacularly from a top spot in terms of educational success because of embracing the market and privatisation of its schools.

In the UK, however, we need look no further than just north of Berwick-upon-Tweed to see a school system and conditions for teachers which reflect much of what the NUT seeks. It is of course incumbent upon trade unionists to be internationalists. There are many struggles at the global level and much to learn from teachers' unions across the world, but a trip to our near neighbour in Scotland offers a refreshing view of what, in many ways, the NUT is fighting to win back for our members and our children.

3

Ofsted's strategy of tension

Louise Regan

I began teaching in 1990, two years after the 1988 Education Reform Act. This Act, introduced by a Conservative government, is widely regarded as the most important piece of education legislation since the 1944 Butler Act. The 1988 Act introduced mechanisms by which schools could be removed from local authority control; the introduction of grant-maintained schools; the introduction of key stages and a national curriculum; the removal of further and higher education from local authority control, and the implementation of local management of schools. This short list of changes has had a significant impact on comprehensive education during the 26 years I have been teaching in primary schools.

Alongside the 1988 Act the inspection of schools was handed to the Office for Standards in Education (Ofsted). Ofsted is a word that brings fear to the hearts of even the strongest and coolest of school leaders. Ofsted has the power to decide the future of any school and it wields this power with a ferocity that at times is alarming. Ofsted has blighted the educational landscape for the whole of my career and has, since its inception, been unpopular with teachers and unions. In its early years Ofsted was considered heavy handed with long inspections, six weeks' notice prior to an inspection and high levels of pressure. Over the years the inspection framework has been reviewed and amended and now schools have just a day's notice before inspectors arrive on their doorstep. The argument for the introduction of such short-or-no notice inspections was that this stopped schools preparing for the six weeks prior to any inspection and therefore reduced the workload and burden in schools. This view is far from a true representation of the realities in our schools.

Most schools are on constant Ofsted alert. In staff meetings, during teacher training (INSET) days and in performance management meetings there are the constant mantras of 'we need this for Ofsted', 'this is what Ofsted requires', and the threat of the school being placed in a category, forced to convert to an academy and the dreadful 'naming and shaming' in the press. Ofsted has tried in more recent times to improve its popularity with the school workforce, producing guidance and myth busters, but as many people in education will know the system is not in any way fair or unbiased and you are at the whim of the inspection team. There continue to be horror stories from schools about the inspection process. 'Rogue inspectors' are – contradictorily – legion. These people try to impose their views on a school, won't listen to the school's views, all too often accusing schools of 'making excuses', and who appear to revel in putting schools in a category to then walk away and leave behind them the chaos that ensues.

Ofsted has been a controversial body throughout its relatively short history. For most of its existence, Ofsted has existed in a state of high tension with schools, mainly because of its willingness to criticise and find fault. At least some of the difficulty was attributed by many to the confrontational Chief Inspector, Chris Woodhead, who ran the Office from 1992 until resignation in 2000. During this time Woodhead pushed for heavy handed accountability measures for schools and the view that there were no excuses for 'failure'. He instigated many ideas that were very unpopular in schools, particularly the policy of 'naming and shaming' failing schools and their staff and the publication of league tables for primary schools. Woodhead also criticised teaching methods in schools saying that teachers were failing children with their 'trendy' teaching methods and blamed them for falling standards in schools, asserting that the way to raise standards was to return to 'old fashioned' methods of teaching. Very early on he claimed that there were 15,000 incompetent teachers in our schools and that they should be sacked. This set the tone for his relationship with the teaching profession throughout his time as chief inspector.

Woodhead's resignation in 2000 was widely celebrated by teachers, who believed that his policies had blamed teachers for standards in schools, ignoring the issue of funding or the impact of poverty. However, the inspection regime he instituted continues to be unpopular and successive chief inspectors have failed to change the profession's view of it. The current but soon-to-depart Chief Inspector, Sir Michael Wilshaw, has continued to be confrontational with teachers and their unions. He was famously quoted as saying that 'if morale in the staffroom was low, the head could be assured he was doing something right.' These comments show to many how completely disconnected with the profession the inspection regime is and also the complete disregard with which they hold teachers. The recent announcement that Amanda Spielman is the favoured candidate to lead the inspection service has done nothing to improve the profession's perception of Ofsted. Amanda Spielman has no teaching experience and following a meeting with the Education Select Committee, members of this body stated that she was unsuitable for the role not least because of her lack of teaching experience. However, the former Secretary of State for Education, Nicky Morgan, stated that she intended to press ahead with the appointment of Amanda Spielman despite the opposition from MPs and teachers. This complete disregard for the profession is something which has festered inside the inspection regime since its inception.

More recently the inspection regime has become caught up in the debate around academies. Schools that are in 'special measures' or which are deemed to 'require improvement' have immense pressure put on them to convert to academies overseen by Multi Academy Trusts (MAT). However, there appears to be no evidence that this measure supports school improvement, in fact the opposite appears to be true. For 'inadequate' schools that become sponsored academies, 12% remain inadequate (1 in 8) compared to just 2% (1 in 50) of those that remain in the local authority maintained sector. This data provided by Ofsted, following a question from Lord Hunt of Kings Heath, casts serious doubt on the view that MATs are the answer to school improvement. This data shows that a school is actually far more likely to improve if it remains in the maintained school sector.

Kevin Courtney, Deputy General Secretary of the National Union of Teachers at the time, stated that:

> '*The Government's whole schools strategy is based on the dogmatic belief that conversion to academy status by definition improves standards. These latest findings show this to be nonsense. It is in fact the proven structural support of maintained schools which is more likely to achieve results. But the Government's educational vandalism is systematically undermining the role of local authorities in education, to the detriment of our children.*'

The inspection process has been widely criticised, particularly by

teachers and teacher unions. They have argued that it causes high
levels of stress among staff under pressure to ensure their schools
perform well. Despite the changes to the Inspection Framework
over time, this stress and pressure continues and schools continue to
raise concerns about the impact of inspections. Past-NUT General
Secretary Christine Blower made the following statement about the
inspection system:

> '*Ofsted is one of the causes of unsustainable levels of pressure and workload for
> teachers, heads and pupils. Teachers are professionals who strive to improve
> teaching and learning in their school, and want to provide the best outcomes for
> their students. School inspection models must assist in this.*
>
> *Teachers need to have confidence in the inspectorate, the reliability of its
> judgements, and its capacity to support schools and promote improvement.*
>
> *Instead, Ofsted is having a negative impact on children's education, disrupting
> important planned activities, and causing additional stress and pressure. It is not
> fit for purpose. What is needed is a new model of school accountability, one that
> involves school self-evaluation and is designed in discussion with the profession.*'

It is difficult to find anyone who speaks positively about Ofsted in
education, but what is often used against teachers and schools is the
threat that their school will fail and that any criticism is just an
excuse for poor teaching or leadership. At its worst extremes Ofsted
has been linked to the suicide of headteachers and teachers
following schools being put into a category. This level of pressure
and the complete sense of failure that is created by the inspection
regime continues to increase and is often cited by teachers as a cause
of stress and anxiety. Even when inspections go well there is often
criticism from schools. It appears that Ofsted continues to be viewed
as a punitive system rather than anything that links to a real
willingness to support school improvement.

Most teachers dread the phone call from Ofsted. They know the
pressure that it puts on their school and that the fate of their school
lies in the hands of a random inspection team. Last year Ofsted
announced that it was getting rid of 40% of its inspectors because
they were 'not up to the job'. There were huge complaints from
unions about this and calls for the judgements of those inspectors to
be reviewed, but nothing was done. They were removed from the
inspectorate and Ofsted continued. There are increasing numbers of

complaints against Ofsted inspections each year, but the complaints are considered by Ofsted themselves rather than by an independent body. As Dr Mary Bousted, General Secretary of the Association of Teachers and Lecturers, stated when she questioned whether Ofsted ought to be dealing with its own complaints:

> *'There's no independent guarantee that it is being done in a rigorous way or that it will change outcomes that were not justified. There is every pressure on Ofsted to hold the line, and not change grades, given that any changes will give critics the evidence to question their judgments.'*

I have been teaching in primary schools for 26 years and have probably endured more inspections than most. My school successfully challenged a negative Ofsted report and had it overturned. I have tales of horror from most inspections I have been through ranging from rude and offensive inspectors to complete incompetence. Inspectors who have told me which reading scheme I should be using, how often I should be observing staff, and trying to trip us up with constant questioning. I understand why teachers and headteachers leave – the pressure in schools is immense and it is increasing on a daily basis. The new primary curriculum and the Standard Assessment Test (SAT) fiasco of 2016 are just another thing that teachers will be blamed for.

Of course we want all schools to be as good as they can. Of course, we want all children to achieve the best that they can, but I know that the way to encourage schools is not to criticise, ridicule or name and shame but to build on their strengths, to provide positive support and good quality professional development, and to respect the diversity of the schools that we have. The education systems that do best do not have high stakes testing regimes, they do not have a punitive inspection regime, but they do have a highly respected and trained education workforce, a well-funded school system, and a broad and balanced curriculum with access to arts, music, drama, outdoor education, humanities, languages and all those subjects which are gradually being driven from our schools.

Ofsted never really had the respect of the teaching profession but these days you struggle to find anyone that sees it as a useful or positive experience. We need to trust teachers and schools. We must allow them to work together collaboratively, to support school development, and any systems to monitor schools should be carried out by practising teachers. They should be about identifying strengths, and where areas for development are identified, funding should be put in place to support this in a positive way. Perhaps then we can start to reduce pressure and workload in schools and retain teachers for the future.

4
Heart and soul of teaching
Siobhan Collingwood

I have always said that my job is the best job in the world; it is my privilege to nurture the joy of learning and enthusiasm of the children entrusted to our care by their parents. Each day I am surrounded by professionals who inspire and motivate both their students and colleagues. It is my daily challenge as a headteacher to create an atmosphere that nurtures and develops the talents and abilities of children and adults by creating a rich and fertile learning environment. We work together, laugh together, sometimes cry together, care together and learn together. My place of work is a place that develops people's intellect, feeds their soul, ignites their creativity and makes their life better; a place with a heart and soul.

After twenty eight years in teaching, I am – for the first time – really fearful for the future of the vocation that I and my colleagues love. As headteacher of my current school for the last eleven years, a school that serves a very disadvantaged community, I do not scare easily. I have comforted parents with nothing left to lose as they hand the care of their child over to the state, asking me to look after their baby and make sure that they have their favourite cuddly toy at bed time. I have faced confrontational parents screaming at me that they are not aggressive and that I am heartless. I have got in between incensed parents on the verge of losing control and visited the homes of children as their lives and the lives of the adults that care for them are imploding. I have attempted to preserve sufficient resources to protect the level of provision that I know is required to achieve high levels of care and attainment for some of the most vulnerable children in our society, as budgets have shrunk, grown, and shrunk again. I have introduced change after change that has been imposed by successive governments, intent on making their mark on public services in the country, using the best of each initiative to enhance our provision and protecting colleagues and children from the worst of each. I have held children as they describe in graphic detail, the ruinous relationships, neglect and fear that blights their lives, about their daily fight for survival that makes me want to wrap them in a blanket and carry them home with me, to a place of warmth, security and love. In all the years of caring for children, parents and my work colleagues, I have always believed that I can chart a course through whatever difficulties arise, guided by a strong moral compass and a belief that my job is to be an advocate for the right of children to a high-quality, rounded and broad education which is enjoyable and prepares them fully for the modern world. For the first time ever I am looking at an educational landscape that is foreign to me, a landscape devoid of warmth, humour and a sense of humanity. I am fearful that neither I or my educational ethos can survive in this landscape. I am scared that as a profession, we are about to lose the heart and soul of education.

Over the years that I have been a teacher I have seen the professionalism of teachers being steadily eroded by a constant stream of initiatives that are vaunted as the new way to ensure that children receive an equitable experience of learning, wherever they live and however wealthy their parents are. Most have been well meaning but many have been ill-researched, non-consultative and not firmly founded in any knowledge of child development or meta cognition. Some have helped teachers to become more disciplined in the framing of units of learning and to measure the progress of children as they learn. The defining and labelling of a national entitlement to learning in the form of a National Curriculum has, when used most successfully, created the warp of a beautiful tapestry of learning, through which the most successful schools have woven the enthusiasms and experiences of the children and teachers in their classrooms and the events within the schools, communities, country and the world. When used least successfully it has created bland, uniform boxes of learning or units of work and a reductive tick box approach that creates a black-and-white, painting-by-numbers approach to learning.

After working with Sir Jim Rose on a review of the National Curriculum, I now watch with sadness as the current format is implemented. In putting together such a crucial and statutory framework for learning it is incomprehensible to me that it ignored the findings of other reviews, including the Cambridge Primary

Review, and it ignored the growing body of knowledge about child development. During its formulation the review ignored its own consultations and the opinion of its own expert panel, half of whom resigned part way through saying that they did not wish to be associated with the emerging programmes of study and that they were being too heavily influenced by Michael Gove and Nick Gibb. It is no surprise therefore that the National Curriculum in its current incarnation is a backward-looking and fundamentally flawed document that does not assist schools in preparing children to live and function in our modern world.

This retrograde and reductive National Curriculum has of course impacted upon the new end of Key Stage Standard Assessment Test (SATs) arrangements in Years 2 and 6. Arrangements have been constantly altered with a drip-feeding of information throughout the school year which has resulted in an absolute lack of clarity about test content gradings and expectations. The resultant stress has meant that many teachers are experiencing elevated levels of anxiety and sleepless nights, sometimes requiring anti-depressant medication.

When the tests were actually delivered, the arrangements were again chaotic, with both Key Stage Spelling and Grammar (SPaG) tests being published on line before hand and Parcel Force pick-ups arranged whilst the tests were underway. At my school, we were monitored on our test security arrangements for the SPaG test, the day after it had been published on line. The papers themselves were ridiculously difficult, dry and irrelevant, with a heavy focus upon the vocabulary that proved to be punitive for our English as an Additional Language (EAL) and disadvantaged pupils. There were tricks throughout the papers that were designed to catch children out and the level of challenge was quite often ridiculously inappropriate for children of this age range, compounded by far too many questions to be completed in an insufficient time scale. The content of the papers often bore hardly any comparison to the practice papers and exemplar material provided by the DfE, a fact commented upon by many of the children as well as the staff. The result was that children ran out of time, cried, felt thick and in some cases had nose bleeds or vomited. Watching children cry and lose confidence, despite all that we have done to build their self esteem is harrowing for any caring teacher and has led many of us to say 'NEVER AGAIN!' I will never do that to children in my care again!

I have had enough of a testing regime that damages our children to this extent. The Government acknowledged the emotional and mental fragility of our nation's children and appointed a Children's Mental Health Champion. She was unceramoniously dumped when she made clear the damaging impact of the current educational policy that creates undue testing pressure from the age of four upwards and that narrowed the curriculum in response to high-stakes accountability systems that measures only the core subjects. When she called for a re-evaluation of our system with a greater focus upon curriculum models that help children to grow, her days were numbered. The Government is not just ignoring her findings in this area; there are many other organisations that they are choosing to ignore:

- The Association of Teachers and Lecturers conducted a survey of primary teachers and 50% of respondents said that they were aware of children in their class who had self-harmed.
- The University of York conducted an international research project into the well-being of young people and, out of 15 sample countries, our children came 13th for all-round well-being and for enjoying school.
- Childline in its most recently publicised figures shows a 13% increase in children referring themselves over exam-led pressures and a 200% increase in children seeking counselling because of exam and test-based stress.
- The National Union of Teachers 'Exam Factory' research showed that 62% of children are very anxious/stressed by SATs/exams and that 88% of children do not like them.

I have watched as the quest for accountability has driven assessment to the front of educational practice, as measuring and weighing has taken the lead. Instead of being a means of quantifying what a child learns and guiding the next steps in their learning journey, tests have become the only reason to 'learn' anything. The content of the tests and how to pass them has become the Holy Grail of education; learning that feeds the intellect and soul and helps humanity to grow has been derided as the preserve of the 'educational blob' and the 'enemies of ambition'. It has become marginalised or extinct in 'successful' schools which are celebrated for driving up educational standards. I despise this simplistic false polarity and rail against the subtext that says that young people cannot achieve high standards whilst being inspired and motivated, that creativity is the opposite of success, and that allowing people time to learn and develop is unambitious.

I reject the view that children progress in straight lines. Any parent knows that child development is a messy thing: children grow new teeth in clusters, with long gaps in between, take backward steps in weaning and potty training, wake you up in the night after sleeping through, before seeming as if they will never emerge from their beds as teenagers. The same is true of them as learners: cognition develops in spurts, with some children having long plateaus before steep growth and others a much more even profile. The current testing regime that tests according to age rather than readiness, or at the discretion of the teacher, is bound to create flawed data and is not employed until the very end of public education in many of the most highly regarded educational systems in the world.

I have watched as data from this flawed system has formed the basis of Office for Standards in Eduction (Ofsted) inspections that use mostly single word gradings from a single framework to define schools whatever the size, catchment, history or circumstances. As a consequence of these simplistic judgements successful schools and teachers are invited to share their expertise with other schools performing less well in these gradings, regardless of the complexities and differences between schools. Further powers for the Department for Education (DfE) and unelected Regional Schools' Commissioners (RSCs) will mean that schools that do not receive a favourable Ofsted grading will be put under pressure to become part of a Multi Academy Trust (MAT) with a sponsor to be decided upon by the RSC. This is so despite recent data that implies that the improvement in schools that are Local Authority (LA) controlled is faster than in schools that are academies – even though joining a MAT is supposed to create more autonomy, and so a greater chance of 'success', for schools.

Now, this flawed data defines schools in increasingly derogatory terms, with completely random levels fixed and defined as floor levels for schools to be judged against. Anybody below these floor levels is deemed to be failing, and under the proposed White Paper will be informed (by Regional School's Commissioners) of their perceived failure and instructed to join a MAT with a sponsor (to be decided upon by the Regional School Commissioner). The Executive Principle of one of the largest MATs has advised schools that are not yet academies, that schools give up a lot of direct control when joining a MAT. Legal services have further advised that once in a MAT, it is next to impossible to leave and that it becomes necessary to fit the brand of that MAT, rather than forge an individualised school culture. As a headteacher who defines the best direction of travel for my school alongside Governors, staff and parents, in line with the needs of the community that I serve, this does not sound like a more autonomous position for our school than we currently experience. Why would I convert to an academy and lose this autonomy?

At present we are a school rated 'good' with some provision that is 'outstanding'. I work alongside my County Schools Advisor, from a County Service with a proven track record in school improvement. Currently 94% of County Council Schools are rated good or outstanding by Ofsted, compared to 83% of academies. Why would I convert to an academy and lose this support? I work with a cluster of over 30 primary schools that share expertise across schools and work very closely together and have the opportunity to visit any school in Lancashire that might be helpful in looking for ways to improve performance further. Why would I convert to an academy and lose this support network?

Yet the Government tells us that it is their goal for all schools to become academies in the next six years. They assure us that the DfE-established systems will do a better job of monitoring and overseeing the work of schools than Local Authorities do at present, and yet this year there has been blunder after blunder. The introduction of assessment without levels and assessment systems has been confused and shambolic. They have had to abandon baseline testing arrangements because they did not listen to the advice given by the profession. They have had to abandon test papers that have been published online before the dates of the tests. They have taken six months longer than other government departments to produce accounts that have then been slammed for mismanagement and lack of financial accountability in academies. Why would I chose to be run directly by a government department that has not proven itself able to manage the responsibilities that it currently oversees, without taking on responsibility for a further 4,000 MATs?

Some principals of academies have been found to draw two or three salaries, to employ members of their families as unqualified staff, to buy their own consultancy services into the schools that they lead, to draw huge salaries (some more than £300,000 per year), even when, in some cases, there have been sharp declines in standards across their schools. Sponsors for the increased numbers of academies are proving difficult to recruit with one leader of a MAT urging an audience of investors to '… go forth, let's all make hay' because 'education is a tremendous sector for financial returns'. Executive salaries, questionable financial practices and an interest in the possibilities for finacial returns off the back of our children's education does not sound appealing to me. At the moment, I work alongside governors from all sectors who, on a totally voluntary basis, oversee the strategic direction of the school. Why would I choose to lose the support of such an altruistic group and swap to a board of trustees, by converting to an academy?

The government is not answering these or any of my questions, simply telling me to stop complaining and making myself feel bad. The recruitment crisis within schools, which is seeing staff resign at unprecedented levels and a large proportion of trainee teachers chosing not to enter the profession, is not being treated seriously. We are simply having more imposed upon us, more damaging changes made to the curriculum and more pressure being placed upon our children to pass increasingly narrow and unattainable tests. The government is not listening to any research or data that casts doubt upon the silver bullet of academisation or that evidences the damage being done to our children. We need to raise the volume!

It is time for us to reclaim our professionalism, to be a powerful advocate for children and to not sleep walk into the disastrous experimentation with privatisation of the education sector that is happening at present. We must work together across unions and across stakeholder groups. I do not want to belong to a generation of teachers that says 'I stood by and let that happen'. It is easy to feel helpless in the face of such fierce dogma being imposed so determinedly but I have been heartened to see schools working together, unions speaking with the same voice, and parents standing full square beside us in a battle being spearheaded in my area, Lancaster and Morecambe.

In recent months, headteachers in our area have shared e-mail chains and attended meetings declaiming the current educational direction of travel, have held public meetings where 200 people at a time have attended to speak out and hear about government policy. Teachers and support staff have attended joint union meetings and given up Saturday mornings to run alternative classrooms that invite members of the public to see how we choose to teach when unshackled from government diktat. We have collected signatures from members of the public during these Saturday stalls and supported parents who have chosen to strike with their children over toxic testing. Instead of maintaining a distance from parents we have told them the truth of how we feel and they have told us their concerns. We are fighting the same fight, a fight to preserve the childhood of children and their right to a broad, balanced and rigorous education that encourages them to become thinkers, creative problem solvers and lifelong learners.

It has been fascinating to watch the 'May 3rd – Let our Kids be Kids' social media group develop in size, influence and understanding. What started as a gut reaction to the experiences of their children's schooling became an informed, educated and powerful group that shared articles, research papers and stories, that attended meetings, spoke up and took action. On the 3rd May 2016, 1,700 children in our local primary schools went on strike to protest about the impact of SATs and inappropriate toxic testing. Many more returned template letters to school saying that even though they were unable to participate, they supported the action. They held festivals of learning in two parks across the area, where children learned through play, with treasure hunts, reading circles, art activities, maths and science. Parents and headteachers have written letters to MPs, met with their MPs and even travelled to London to lobby their local MPs in Parliament. The resulting press interest has been significant and as a consequence when speaking to members of the public on the Saturday stalls it is very rare to find somebody who is not aware of the issues.

This all grew over a period of two to three weeks. The same group is determined to continue opposing the current testing regime, its strangulation of the curriculum and the linked policy of universal academisation. They are planning to encourage parents to insist that their child's school does not teach children to pass Key Stage 1 and 2 tests from September, as they do not want them to sit them. Headteachers and teachers are encouraging staff in their own and other schools to vote and participate in the industrial action organised by the NUT against the government's proposals. Festivals of Learning will be run by teachers on strike day, in public places, to which children will be invited to attend and teachers will inform members of the public of the damage being done to our children's education. Parents are working with unions, staff in schools and headteachers. It feels like a real movement is growing that can make a determined stand to oppose current educational policy. Together we are a strongly principled, well informed, very large and powerful group. If this model is replicated across the country I believe that the government will be forced to listen.

Recent months and developments in our area have given me hope, I am not as scared for the educational vocation that I love. In our area and others across the country we are not standing by, we are not sleep walking into disaster, we have stopped complying and making idiotic and corrupt policies work. Now is the time for every teacher in the country to take a stand for what they believe in, this is the fight of a generation and a fight for the heart and soul of education. Stop toxic testing, let's never do that to children again. Stop selling off the education of our children to the highest bidder! Enough is Enough!

5

Tested to destruction
Tests, trust and education

Alan Gibbons

In December 2011, a *Guardian* editorial concluded that:

> *'English children are now the most tested children in the industrialised world (thanks to devolution, their Scottish and Welsh cousins do not suffer the same burden of examination); the average pupil will be subjected to at least seventy tests during his or her school career.'*

The same article found that 'spending on exam fees nearly doubled, to over £300m, between 2002 and 2010'. While we are talking about money, many millions of pounds have been spent on Standard Assessment Tests (SATs) crammers, curriculum guides and sample test papers, all of this directed at children younger than eleven years old. Primary schools, since autumn 1989, have been railroaded into a culture of permanent tension in which the school year is punctuated by various forms of high stakes national tests. Children are variously prepared, prepped, cajoled, urged, occasionally bribed, even (quite rarely, thanks to the vigilance of schools) bullied and exhorted to ever greater efforts to secure results which might, just might, keep the Ofsted wolf from the staffroom door.

In 2009, a Cambridge University review of primary education described national testing as 'the elephant in the curriculum', and noted that in the final year of primary school 'breadth competes with the much narrower scope of what is to be tested'. Notoriously, this led to art lessons and sports activities such as swimming being cancelled, the entire primary curriculum thrown into imbalance in pursuit of something called 'test excellence'. In his book *Education by Numbers: The Tyranny of Testing*, Warwick Mansell explains how a strategy of 'pursuing results almost as ends in themselves has been forced on schools, in their desperation to fulfil the requirements of hyper-accountability'. But, he writes, 'this grades race is ultimately self-defeating. It does not guarantee better educated pupils, just better statistics for schools and the government.'

So let's take a look at the primary testing regime, how we got here, how it has affected children, and whether there are alternatives to the present arcane and self-defeating regime. Now, ask any trainee teacher and she or he will tell you that there are two forms of assessment:

* Formative assessments *are continuous feedback that can be used by teachers to improve their teaching and by their pupils to improve their learning. These assessments are locally administered, deployed by the teacher, and used as they see fit. They help students identify their strengths and weaknesses and target areas that need work. They involve a process of discussion and have a strong element of teacher autonomy.*

*Summative assessments *evaluate student learning at the end of a specific period to determine if children have learned what they are meant to learn; are evaluative rather than diagnostic; are often recorded in scores or grades. They are often administered at a national level and used for political purpose. There is little teacher autonomy and little local discussion between teacher and pupil. Instead, teachers, schools and pupils tend to be graded and raw scores reported to parents and the public.*

Traditionally, the balance has tilted more towards formative assessment in the early years and shifted rather more towards summative assessment the closer children come to school leaving age, when prospective employers are looking for evidence of candidates' ability to do a particular job. No teacher is opposed to assessment. Teachers since the year dot have used a mixture of formative and summative assessment. The question was how best to assess progress. That meant deciding whether it was in the best interests of the child; whether it merited the time and effort; whether it caused stress; whether it contributed to the child's progress. The arbiter of this decision was the teacher, and the mentor of the decision process an experienced head teacher. From the moment Margaret Thatcher's Education Minister, Kenneth Baker, took office in 1985, the whole way schools assessed children swung dramatically in the direction of high stakes, publicly reported, summative testing, as much for infant and junior children as for adolescents. The teacher became the conduit of national priorities, the head teacher the supervisor of the teacher drones' efforts. Summative testing had arrived in the hitherto relatively progressive world of British primary education.

Kenneth Baker introduced a controversial 'National Curriculum' through the 1988 Education Act. The purpose of the National Curriculum was to standardise the content taught across schools. Children would be tested, regardless of any stress generated, and the results compiled in league tables detailing the assessment statistics for each school. Parents would be able to use these league tables to choose a school for their children. This was the thin end of a very thick wedge, which would eventually lead to academies, free schools and an education market. Assessments known as Standard Assessment Tests (SATs) would take place at the end of three 'Key Stages', at ages seven, eleven and fourteen. The first, best-known and most enduring element in the apparatus of national testing had arrived, and what a gargantuan cuckoo it turned out to be, propelling much that had characterised good practice out of the pedagogic nest.

Post-war British primary education prior to the 1980s has often been described as 'the envy of the world'. Child-centred learning was to the fore. There was an accent on play and exploration. The experience of the child and her or his ability to test hypotheses in practice were central. The notion that the child was a passive receptacle into which learning was to be poured was widely rejected. Unobtrusive diagnostic activities became prevalent. Inspections were relatively benign and, with the end of the eleven plus examination and selection in most parts of the country, assessment was largely the preserve of the classroom teacher. The traditionalist Black Papers and a furore about William Tyndale School in London, in 1976, had built up a head of steam behind a 'back to basics' counter-revolution. It came to a head with Baker. In April 1991, the first round of the new nationwide Standard Attainment Tests was labelled 'unfair and unworkable' by many primary school teachers. The tests were introduced over a period of several years, 1991–1998, going through a number of changes.There were tests in Maths, English and Science at age seven and eleven in primary schools, and at age fourteen in secondary schools. This article concentrates on the primary school experience.

Stories with unhappy beginnings often continue along a path haunted by enduring misery. So it was with the SATs. They were unpopular with children, teachers and parents from the beginning, with many parents supporting a short-lived teacher boycott, ended largely because only one union, the National Union of Teachers, pursued it consistently. As early as 1991, in a sign of things to come, the government had to revise the structure of the tests, reducing attainment targets, and promising that the new tests would be less time consuming and more manageable for teachers. In April 1993, a review led by Sir Ron Dearing slimmed down the requirements of the national curriculum even further. A pattern was set. Politicians declared the new system a boon to parents and a guarantor of rising standards. Children resented it or went along with it because they were powerless to do anything else. Some parents withdrew their children. Teaching unions and academic bodies fiercely criticised the new set-up. Rather than listen to their concerns, government would trim and tack, desperate to preserve the Frankenstein monster it had created even though each new 'reform' hollowed out the original system.

By October 1995, Standard Assessment Tests were in crisis. Half of school children sitting the required English and Maths tests failed to reach the target grade. With the advent of the new Labour government in 1997, headed by Tony 'education, education, education' Blair, change might have been expected. Change there was, but it wasn't the dismantling of the creaking monolith. Instead, the new Secretary of State for Education, the combative David Blunkett, set new targets for SATs scores, expecting 80 per cent of 11-year-old children to achieve the 'average' level four in their English tests by 2002. There was no peer-reviewed, compelling evidence to show that increased testing enhanced learning. Even when results stubbornly failed to rise as predicted, New Labour ploughed on, continuing along the Tory path. In an absolute hoot, it introduced literacy and numeracy hours to focus how pupils were taught.

Though test results in English and Numeracy finally started to show very modest improvements, it can be argued that much of this was due to 'teaching to the test', a criticism that came to pursue each new Education Secretary like one of the Erinyes, the Greek gods of vengeance. Teachers became good at anticipating questions and drilling the children in how to answer them while, simultaneously, England and Wales fared poorly in international comparisons. The literacy hour was soon treated with ridicule and contempt. Its four sections, especially the notorious plenary, constituted a ludicrously inept response to children's needs, and was eventually quietly dropped without any serious explanation, analysis or apology. Ask as the educational community might, it never elicited a proper admission of the financial cost of this fiasco. By 2000, a revised national curriculum had to be introduced. Yes, the reform to end reforms was being reformed. The government designated the year 'Maths Year 2000', launching a campaign to interest children in maths and raise attainment.

Fads, revisions, alterations and acrobatic contortions proliferated. Primary teachers might remember that there were trials of history, geography and technology SATs involving hat designing, beautiful photos of chalk cliffs, and Cluedo heads of Guy Fawkes and King James I. Teachers trialled the tests; then, after hours of work, they were quietly dropped. Again, there was no analysis, no apology, no admission of cost. The speaking and listening strategy came and went with its expensive videos and information packs, delivered to schools in crisp cellophane wrappers and soon to vanish into cupboards or, more likely, bins, landing on top of the nine ring-bound folders of the deceased curriculum. Teachers tested children's reading with a translucent overlay sheet, which had the texture of the notorious toilet paper 'Izal'. The teacher got the child to read a hundred words from a selected picture book. There was a national list. You couldn't use an unauthorised text. Heaven forfend! The child was allowed eight errors. If she or he made nine she was reading below the desired level and a suitable case for remediation. Who would have known that a single word contained such lethal power? There was the floating and sinking test at age seven, which saw several tonnes of bananas disintegrate and many stones nestle truculently at the bottom of tanks, but at least this was an attempt at scientific investigation. Science investigations evolved after some time into pencil and paper activities listing alleged 'science facts', a rather unscientific concept in itself, and soon amounted to a memory test. These, too, went the way of the legendary nine subject curriculum, which vanished like the morning mist, unanalysed, uncosted and unmourned.

In September 2001, Wales and Northern Ireland scrapped league tables, preferring systems of ongoing assessment. In December of that year, schools failed to achieve the government's target of 75 per cent of all 11-year-olds reaching level 4 in Maths, dipping by one percentage point to 71 per cent. Ofsted claimed teacher shortages were to blame. The government set new targets, aiming for an 80 per cent level four pass rate by 2002 and 85 per cent by 2006. Some advisors started talking comically about all children being above average in this brave new world, exhibiting a curious definition of what is average. In neo-Stalinist fashion, failure was met with exhortation to work harder, teacher generals, and dragoon your child troops to ever greater efforts at the chalk face to produce the ever elusive 'high' standards.

In August 2002, schools failed to meet the expected level four pass rate of 80 per cent. All those booster groups, Stakhanovite 'leading' literacy and numeracy teachers, all the permanent tracking and testing, analyses of children 'on the cusp of level four' and so on, failed to shift the stubbornly resistant test scores. The latest Great Leader at the Department for Education would swim in the Yangtze of drill, grade and fail, and sank. At that time, I launched Authors Against the SATs, supported by the likes of Philip Pullman, Michael Rosen, Anne Fine and hundreds more, to expose the way the tests failed children, marginalised real learning through experimentation, open-ended investigation and play, and fell short of the government's expectations, even in the game of raw data. Did these multiple failures mean that anyone in the Department for Education for a moment wondered whether the whole dismal experience might be the cause of a fundamental rethink? Sadly, no. The Conservatives introduced SATs, Labour continued them and, when the Tories returned to office, they not only retained the whole shebang, but also added a new raft of tests, each more arcane than the last.

Cambridge University carried out a two-year inquiry into English primary schools. Other parts of the UK and countries such as France, Norway, Finland and Japan used testing but it was 'less intrusive, less comprehensive, and considerably less frequent', Cambridge's Primary Review concluded.

England was unique in using testing to prescribe what was taught in schools, to monitor teaching standards, and to encourage parents to choose schools based on the results of the tests, according to Kathy Hall from the National University of Ireland in Cork, and Kamil Ozerk, from the University of Oslo, who conducted the research.

'Assessment in England, compared to our other reviewed countries, is pervasive, highly consequential, and taken by officialdom and the public more generally to portray objectively the actual quality of primary education in schools,' their report concluded in 2008.

Most disreputably of all, this entire oppressive apparatus was always judged by the inspection service, Ofsted, part of the government's own educational establishment, not by independent research. In the same period that the SAT blizzard blew and cracked its cheeks, according to the Organization for Economic Co-operation and Development (OECD) Programme for International Student Assessment (Pisa) global survey of 15-year-olds, Britain slipped from fourth to 16th in science, seventh to 25th in literacy, and eighth to 28th in maths. There are problems with the Pisa methodology, which I don't examine here, but the point is that when any yardstick other than Ofsted conclusions was used to evaluate the testing regime, it came up short.

The OECD's Economic Survey 2011 pointed out that, in the previous decade, improvements in educational outcomes stuttered, bolstered only by grade inflation. The OECD reported that 'high-stake tests' grew like Topsy in England, but were only able to 'produce perverse incentives' and 'lead to negligence of non-cognitive skill formation'. Teachers worked ever harder, but in thrall to a dubious pedagogy that hindered their efforts. In contrast, Finland featured consistently in the upper reaches of the Pisa rankings. It had no league tables, no school inspections or publicly reported tests comparing pupils. The first test of this kind that Finnish children took was at school leaving age. The Finnish government carried out sampling, for internal use only, not for national publication. Teachers there were well trained, well paid, and had a high social status and considerable autonomy. Compare that to British teachers, who were forever demonised by Education Secretaries, the media and Ofsted, even though any failings were not their own, but the product of their hobbling by a theoretically incoherent and ever-changing body of educational policy. In *Moby Dick* fashion, the government's course was right because the latter-day Ahab, in the form of the Education Minister, said it was, not because the educational community had been able to provide any robust evidence to justify successive governments' claims. Indeed, by the time of Michael Gove's tenure as Secretary State for Education, people who had spent a lifetime in schools and colleges were characterised as 'The Blob', a term as offensive as it is irrelevant to the progress of the UK's schools.

Albert Einstein is alleged to have said that the definition of insanity is doing something over and over again and expecting a different result. By that yardstick, few Education Secretaries post-Baker would escape the charge of insanity. SATs were like a great, beached whale. Department for Education worker bees hacked at it, administered medicine, tried flotation aids, but the poor beast still failed to negotiate the waves with confidence. So what do you do if all else fails? Simple, you add new levels of testing. Enter, stage right, the Key Stage 2 English grammar, punctuation and spelling test. This assumed that there was a universally agreed definition of grammar and that understanding of it would be best achieved by decontextualised cramming of technical terms formerly used in secondary education or college. The 'Spag' test became a box-ticking, right-or-wrong-answer, ailing dolphin, swimming painfully alongside the fading whale of SATs. Suddenly, there was a whole new vocabulary. 'Connectives' were out. 'Conjunctions' were in. Complex sentences were so yesterday. Fronted adverbials were the jaunty young thing prancing out of the Department for Education. Determiners were all the rage. Children would learn to write, not by reading books and discovering models by which they could express themselves, but by learning technical terms sometimes associated with advanced linguistics, not by working with teachers to discover the best way to express meaning, but by being drilled in the intricacies of an arbitrarily-decided grammatical orthodoxy. The state of permanent tension in primary schools was screwed to breaking point with hit squads seeking out any establishment that might be coasting. Prerequisites of success in any human activity, happiness and security, were flung into the fiery furnace along with any conception of trust in the teaching community.

The rollercoaster ride did not end there. Next up in the cavalcade was the Year One phonics test. The Rose Review is widely assigned the key role in introducing synthetic phonics, called by Schools Minister Nick Gibb a tried and tested way of ensuring that every child can read. Unfortunately for Mr Gibb, there is a large body of evidence that even in countries with highly consistent orthography, there are substantial numbers of children who struggle with reading in spite of synthetic phonics programmes. What the Rose Review actually recommended, if it is quoted beyond the sound bite, was:

> *'phonics being taught in the context of a broad, rich language curriculum with lots of experience of good quality literature.'*

Without the second element, the first element is unlikely to be effective. So six-year-olds, with relatively little reading experience, have to do a 'Phonics Screening Check' (PSC) where they 'decode' 30 real words, and 10 nonsense words. If children fail to reach the pass mark, parents and carers must be informed. The Organization for Economic Co-operation and Development found that: 'enjoyment of reading has a greater impact on a child's educational achievement than their parents' socio-economic status'. Instead of pursuing a strategy combining knowledge of the alphabetic system and the phonemes that constitute part of the mechanics of reading with constant immersion in quality fiction, non-fiction and poetry, song and word play, jokes, puzzles and games, the kind of combination recognisable to most able readers, Ministers add another layer of testing, another thumbscrew of pressure, another raft of reporting. On the scales of assessment, the summative pan weighs ever heavier on younger and younger children.

This brings us to the baseline assessment tests. Yes, not satisfied with introducing a phonics test for six-year-olds, the latest Secretary of State, Nicky Morgan, fixed four-year-olds in her sights, introducing one-to-one teacher interviews of children, assessing basic reading ability, numeracy and writing, as well as children's social and emotional development. They take place six weeks after children start school and involve some thirty hours of lesson time and administration. In a National Union of Teachers' survey, 59 per cent of teachers said the tests had disrupted the start of school for Reception children. 31.5 per cent of teachers said the results were an accurate reflection of the children's ability.

Association of Teachers and Lecturers general secretary Mary Bousted said:

'It is questionable how far any form of assessment can accurately show the knowledge and skills of a four-year-old. Children are not robots and do not develop at a regular rate, so we have grave concerns about the reliability of measuring their progress from age four to 11.'

According to former NUT General Secretary Christine Blower, the test is:

'unfair, it's not accurate, it's completely fallible. This set of results is a house built on sand, and the government really should reconsider.'

A Department for Education spokesperson said:

'As part of our mission to deliver educational excellence everywhere, we want to see all children pushed to reach their potential. In order to do that, and to recognise the achievements of schools in the most challenging areas, we want to measure the progress that all pupils make as well as their overall attainment. That means ensuring we have a robust and fair baseline from which to measure that progress.'

Therein lies the thinking of UK governments since the mid-1980s. Children must be pushed, stretched. Schools must live in a permanent tension of testing, tracking and data collection. Everything must be evaluated, nothing left to trust. Forget that teachers are pouring out of the profession, disillusioned by the ever more reductive experience of schooling and the ever increasing workload. Forget that levels of stress among children and teachers are high. Forget that countries such as Finland do it another way and achieve higher Pisa results as a consequence.

There are alternatives, many of them, but this government and the one preceding it, have ignored all evidence that contradicted their attachment to test-obsessive teaching. The question is never 'how do we encourage the children to know more?', but 'how do we test what they know, rank it, order it and publish it?' The former is a commitment to a shared learning experience, the latter the imposition of a top-down evaluation, its end point decided on political grounds. This can be seen in the obsession with advertising learning objectives at the start of lessons. This is fundamentally bad pedagogy. In what genuine learning experience do you know the destination before you embark? Surely, education is about setting out on a journey whose end point is as yet undiscovered.

A European report, 'Education, Audiovisual and Culture Executive Agency, 2009', points to a different approach:

> *'For example, schools in Bulgaria can organise school tests in any subject and at any time they deem appropriate. Similarly in The Netherlands, in which schools for both primary and secondary education are highly autonomous, the testing of pupils is subject to few official regulations. In nearly all schools, a particular form of assessment will be used to determine whether pupils have reached the level normally expected after a fixed period, and the schools themselves will decide how this should be done... In Iceland, there is no standardisation of pupil assessment as practised by different schools and teachers, and the progress of pupils is also reported in many different ways.'*

The fascination with external testing of young children is a recent imposition:

> *'Except in a few countries, national testing is a relatively new form of pupil assessment in Europe. The introduction and use of national tests began slowly and sporadically, and has increased significantly only since the 1990s ... In the great majority of European countries, the aggregated results of national tests for each school are not publicised. In some countries, official documents state clearly that national tests cannot be used to rank schools. This applies to Belgium (the French Community), France in the case of evaluations-bilans (summative assessments), Luxembourg, Austria and Slovenia. In Finland, there was strong pressure from the media to publish school rankings, but the national consensus in the ensuing debate was against publicising test results.'*

In summary, standardised, high-stakes testing, nationally published to grade and judge children, schools and teachers is a recent arrival on the educational stage. Once upon a time in the classroom, we did things differently. This system has been introduced without reliable and robust research, and has been less successful in the available international comparison data than more relaxed assessment regimes. It is not a reliable way to raise standards, help children learn, and give parents information. It is a systematic form of control that reduces education to the collection of data. It causes widespread stress among children, parents and teachers without verifiable positive results, and has cost billions of pounds to little discernible advantage. The burden of testing has been piled on younger and younger shoulders. It is a broken system in which our children are tested to distraction, if not destruction. Everyone who cares about education should redouble their efforts to find a different way.

6

Testing and mental ill health
Nadia Whittome

A study by the United Nations Children's Emergency Fund (UNICEF) compares the well-being of children and young people across 29 of the world's richest countries and, on closer inspection, provides a causal link between poor educational attainment and low overall well-being.[1] The study exposes the United Kingdom as ranking at 24 for 'education', surpassing only Italy, Spain, United States, Greece and Romania. And, at 15.8 for 'overall well-being', falling behind most other European countries. Something is not working in our schools, and for our children.

Of those countries placed within the highest 10 for 'overall well-being' (Netherlands, Norway, Iceland, Finland, Sweden, Germany, Luxembourg, Switzerland, Belgium and Ireland respectively), six were also ranked within the highest ten for 'education' (Netherlands, Belgium, Germany, Finland, Norway and Iceland). It would appear that these countries are on track with 'education' and 'overall well-being'. Educationists who oppose over-testing and the UK government's austerity agenda have suggested that there is a causal link between the two: that increased testing negatively affects both children's mental health and educational attainment.[2]

Why is it that young people in the UK are comparatively less happy? It is well known that young people universally are subjected to increased pressures, including economic, societal, school, friendship and family pressures. Many of the pressures are an inevitable result of a rapidly changing world and form part of growing up. However, any government policy affecting people's lives will also affect children. In the UK we have an economic agenda dominated by ideologically-driven austerity measures that cripples families, and an education policy that is similarly ideologically driven.

Ten per cent of young people aged 5-16 suffer mental ill health,[3] with evidence that mental health problems have increased among young people. The pressure to achieve in school work and tests/examinations is cited among the causes.[4] ChildLine's annual report informed that school and educational problems were related directly to suicidal thoughts:

> '*The pressure and stress of exams and not being able to deal with failure was another reason young people wanted to escape, seeing suicide as their only option.*'[5]

It is worth noting that the self-harm and suicide rate is higher in highly commercialised and intensive school settings such as South Korea, the suicide capital of the world for the 15 to 25 years age group. And, according to Organisation for Economic Co-Operation and Development (OECD) statistics from 2012, in Korea young people were identified as having the lowest quality of life.[6]

There is no doubt that assessment is an important part of learning, but there is a difference between assessment and testing. Test-focused teaching detracts from learning and frequent data gathering and scrutiny of pupils' progress, used to target individual students – particularly those who are 'borderline' – is a source of stress for children and teachers alike.[7]

Although mental health conditions remain most common in secondary schools, children are diagnosed at an increasingly young age.[8] It seems that this can be attributed, at least in part, to excessive testing, with 76 per cent of primary teachers and 94 per cent of secondary teachers agreeing that:

> '*Some pupils in this school have developed stress-related conditions around the time of SATs/public exams.*'[9]

One teacher reported that:

> '*a Year 6 pupil turned to physical self-harming which she attributed to the pressure she felt to achieve a level similar to that of her peers, and to hit a Level 4 in her SATs (she is severely dyslexic and an incredibly hard worker).*'[10]

Mental ill health at school is helped with appropriate teaching that promotes strong relationships with teachers and peers, and which strengthens the voice of the student. Some teachers have reported that the combination of pressure to improve test and exam outcomes for their class, and their increasing workload and stress, has reduced the quality of their relationships with students, and especially with those who are most in need of their time.[11]

The UK government's introduction of high stakes linear exams at GCSE and A Level exacerbates the problem of schools becoming exam factories. Increasingly, children and young people see the main purpose of schooling as gaining qualifications, because this is what schools focus on.[12] This trend has been widely deplored, including by universities and employers, who have argued that the current exam system does not prepare children for life beyond school.[13] All testing creates a high state of anxiety, and it is easy for the needs of those with learning difficulties, emotional difficulties, and/or other social disadvantages to be overlooked. It is not difficult to see how the cycle of stressed teachers and stressed parents will result in the child having no place to escape. It is no wonder that our children are nurturing the time bomb of mental ill health, and that the UK's place in the world league table of education is falling.

Pupils' scores are often unfairly used not only to judge children, their schools and teachers, but also to enforce ideological educational reform by way of 'academisation'. Ultimately, standardised testing is a means of assessing a school and teachers, not children, and certainly should not be used for very young children.

The issue of standardised testing has long dominated the educational reform discussion in the UK. Testing has been justified to head teachers as a method of improving attainment by measuring pupil progress, the attainment of particular groups, and identifying attainment gaps between those in each group and their peers. However, once the gap has been identified, there seems no accompanying remedy to close it. Testing does not reduce the increasing attainment gap between disadvantaged pupils and their peers. Instead, disadvantaged children who have lower attainment than their peers are under greater pressure to meet targets and can become disaffected as a result of their experience of 'failure'. Increased testing can therefore intensify discontent amongst already disadvantaged groups, particularly those with special needs.[14]

Pupils with special educational needs already struggle to reach age-related expectations and often fare better in subjects other than Maths and English, therefore these pupils are disproportionately affected by testing. Furthermore, the focus on academic subjects means that students miss out on other subjects, depriving them of experiencing 'all-round education' that fosters the talents and skills of all students. Forty per cent of children with learning difficulties also suffer mental ill health.[15] It would appear that when children have special educational needs, the unspoken question is whether the child is worth 'investing' in, and whether their grades positively affect school league tables.[16] A measurement of a school's success ought to be whether pupils are engaged in learning creatively and happily, and whether at the end of their period in that school they move on successfully to other educational establishments or to work (if it is available), and contribute effectively as members of society.

When discussing standardised testing, it is impossible not to reflect on the 'academisation' and 'marketisation' of our education system. These are inextricably linked and children have become commodities in a world where education can effectively be bought and sold, with the credible prospect of creating wealth for those who are selling.

Along with living at home, young people spend the majority of their time at school, and the social and emotional health and development of children and young people should be a key priority for all those involved in education. In fulfilling this obligation, it is important that schools employ teaching and assessment models that do not damage young people's mental health. I have spoken to a number of teachers who share this view and would like more autonomy in the classroom, but opposition arises ultimately from government and it is almost impossible for individual schools to challenge. 'Academisation' makes schools work like separate businesses, breaking up the collective power of schools operating within a local authority. Recognising the prevalence of mental ill health, schools should also have pastoral care staff and counsellors. However, budget cuts make this increasingly difficult, and it does not necessarily result in a higher Ofsted rating.

It is striking that countries ranking the highest in 'overall well-being' test their children less. Alternatives to standardised testing are as much about a shift in thinking as they are a practical approach. In particular, the curriculum for young children should be reviewed and revised to take into account all that research has shown about the developmental needs of this age group, and there should be a renewed focus on a broadly-based curriculum that fosters creativity, curiosity and enthusiasm to learn. Collaboration should be encouraged, rather than competition.

It is the type of testing that causes problems for our children and schools, not assessment. Assessment to measure a pupil's progress should not be used to also test teachers and provide school accountability. There are alternatives to testing proposed by educationists that are not used in the UK. For example, 'portfolio-based assessment' uses a collection of pupils' work and tracks progress throughout the school year. This allows each pupil to reflect on selected work to consider what they have learned and their learning process, which contributes to the overall goal of student learning. Another concept is that of 'stealth-assessment' that uses educational computer games to collect data during a student's leisure time. An alternative is to simply use more regular lower stakes testing, rather than high-pressure exams.[17]

In The Netherlands, a compulsory multiple-choice aptitude test takes place at the end of primary school at age twelve. At the end of secondary school The Netherlands has additional testing for those pupils who wish to attend university. These are the only compulsory tests for schoolchildren. Day to day, pupils experience continuous assessment through oral, homework and classroom assignments that are diagnostic in nature, checking a pupil's understanding and providing support where necessary.[18]

For the sake of our children's mental health and the future of a society that values the participation of all individuals, it is time to acknowledge that the current approach of over-testing is not working, and it is time to try something else.

Notes

1. UNICEF. (2013) *Report Card 11. Child Well-being in Rich Countries: A comparative overview.*
2. National Union of Teachers. (2015) *Exam factories?: The impact of accountability measures on children and young people.*

3. Young Minds. (Undated) *Mental health statistics.* [Online] [Accessed: 14th May 2016].

4. Bennett, R. & Burgess, K. (2015) True scale of child mental health crisis uncovered. *The Times.* [Online] 12th March. [Accessed: 16th May 2016].

5. NSPCC. (2015) *'Always there when I need you' ChildLine Review: What's affected children in March 2014 to April 2015,* Page 37.

6. Herald, T.K. (2015) *South Korea still has top OECD suicide rate.* [Online] [Accessed: 17th May 2016].

7. National Union of Teachers. (2015) *Exam factories?: The impact of accountability measures on children and young people.* Page 24.

8. ibid Page 59.

9. ibid

10. ibid

11. ibid Page 5.

12. ibid Page 61.

13. Garner, R. (2014) Schools are becoming 'exam factories' which don't equip students for the world of work, claims CBI. *The Independent.* [Online] 17th January. [Accessed: 18th May 2016].

14. National Union of Teachers. (2015) *Exam factories?: The impact of accountability measures on children and young people.* Page 4.

15. United Kingdom. Foundation for People with Learning Disabilities. (2002) *Count Us In. The Report of the Committee of Inquiry into Meeting the Mental Health Needs of Young People with Learning Disabilities.* London.

16. National Union of Teachers. (2015) *Exam factories?: The impact of accountability measures on children and young people.* Page 62.

17. Peterson, B. & Neill, M. (Undated) *Alternatives to Standardized Tests.* [Online] [Accessed: 1st May 2016].

18. NCCE. (2015) *Instructional systems.* [Online] [Accessed: 11th May 2016].

7
Lies, damned lies and Ofsted's pseudostatistics

Philip Moriarty

Former Secretary of State for Education, Michael Gove, has been variously described as incredibly unpopular, a hate figure, utterly ruthless, and a 'toxic liability'.[1] And that was by his colleagues in the Coalition. (Allegedly.) Those who shared his simple-minded, wilfully uninformed and proto-Victorian views on education, including a certain Richard Littlejohn[2], saw Gove's unpopularity as arising simply because he was driving through what they considered to be essential reforms of an ailing education system.

Just why are Littlejohn and his ilk so certain that the English education system is, as they'd have it, going to hell in a handcart? A very large part of the reason is that they naively, quaintly, yet dangerously assume that education is equivalent to a competitive sport where schools, teachers, and children can be accurately assessed on the basis of positions in league tables. What's worse – and this is particularly painful for a physicist or, indeed, anyone with a passing level of numeracy, to realise – is that this misplaced and unscientific faith in the value of statistically dubious inter-school comparisons is at the very core of the assessment culture of the Office for Standards in Education, Children's Services and Skills (Ofsted).

An intriguing aspect of the swansong of Gove's career as Education Secretary was that he more than once 'butted heads' with Michael Wilshaw,[3] head of Ofsted. One might perhaps assume that this was a particularly apposite example of 'the enemy of mine enemy is my friend'. Unfortunately, not. Ofsted's entirely flawed approach to the assessment of schools is in many ways an even bigger problem than Gove's misplaced attempts to rewind education to the halcyon, but apocryphal, days of yore. Moreover, Gove's gone. Ofsted appears not to be going anywhere any time soon.

I've always been uncomfortable about the extent to which number-abuse and pseudostatistics might be underpinning Ofsted's school assessment procedures. But it was only when I became a parent governor for my children's primary school, Middleton Primary and Nursery School in Nottingham, that the shocking extent of the statistical innumeracy at the heart of Ofsted's processes became clear. (I should stress at this point that the opinions about Ofsted expressed below are mine, and mine alone.)

Middleton is a fantastic school, full of committed and inspirational teachers. But, like the vast majority of schools in the country, it is subject to Ofsted's assessment and inspection regime. Ofsted's implicit assumption is that the value of a school like Middleton, and, by extension, the value of the teachers and students in that school, can be reduced to a set of objective and robust 'metrics' which can in turn be used to produce a quantitative ranking (i.e. a league table). Even physicists, who spend their career wading through reams of numerical data, know full well that not everything that counts can be counted. (By the way, I use the adjective 'inspirational' unashamedly. And because it winds the likes of Littlejohn and Toby Young up. As, I'd imagine, does starting a sentence with a conjunction and ending it with a preposition.)

But let's leave the intangible and unquantifiable aspects of a school's teaching to one side and instead critically consider the extent to which Ofsted's data and processes are, to use that cliché beloved of government ministers, fit for purpose. In its advice to governors,[4] Ofsted – rather ironically, as we'll see – stresses the key importance of objective data and highlights that the governing board should assess the school's performance on the basis of a number of measures which are 'helpfully' summarised at websites such as the Ofsted Data Dashboard and RAISE Online.

Ofsted's advice to governors tacitly assumes that the data it provides, and the overall assessment methodology which gives rise to those data, are objective and can be used to robustly monitor the performance of a given school against others. Let's just take a look at the objective evidence for this claim.

During the governor training sessions I attended, I repeatedly asked to what extent the results of Ofsted inspections (and other

Ofsted-driven assessment schemes) were reproducible. In other words, if we repeated the inspection with a different set of inspectors, would we get the same result? If not, in what sense could Ofsted claim that the results of an inspection were objective and robust? As you might perhaps expect, I singularly failed to get a particularly compelling response to this question. This was for a very good reason: *the results of Ofsted inspections are entirely irreproducible.* A headline from the *Telegraph* in March 2014 said it all: 'Ofsted inspections: You'd be better off flipping a coin'.[5] This was not simply media spin. The Policy Exchange think-tank report, *Watching the Watchmen,* on which the article was based, actually goes further: 'In fact, overall the results are worse than flipping a coin'.[6]

It's safe to say that the think-tank in question, Policy Exchange, is on the right of the political spectrum. It is also perhaps not entirely coincidental that one of its founding members was a certain Michael Gove, and that the Policy Exchange report on Ofsted was highlighted by the right-of-centre press during the period of spats between Wilshaw and Gove mentioned above. None of that, however, detracts from the data cited in the report. These resulted from the work of Robert Coe and colleagues at Durham University and stemmed from a detailed study involving more than 3,000 teachers. Coe has previously criticised Ofsted's assessment methods in the strongest possible terms, arguing that they are not 'research-based or evidence-based'.[7]

Ofsted asks governors to treat its data as objective and make conclusions accordingly. However, without a suitable 'control' study – which in this case is as simple as running independent assessments of the same class with different inspectors – the data on inspections simply cannot be treated as objective and reliable. In this sense, Ofsted is giving governors, schools, and, more generally, the public exceptionally misleading messages.

But it gets worse …

The lack of rigour in Ofsted's inspections is just one part of the problem. It's compounded in a very worrying way by the shocking abuse of statistics that forms the basis of the Data Dashboard and RAISE Online. Governors are presented with tables of data from these websites and asked to make 'informed' decisions on the basis of the numbers therein. This, to be blunt, is a joke.

It would take a lengthy series of artciles to highlight the very many flaws in Ofsted's approach to primary and secondary school data. Fortunately, those posts have already been written by a teacher who has to deal with Ofsted's nonsense on what amounts to a daily basis. I thoroughly recommend that you head over to the *Icing On The Cake*[8] blog and see for yourselves.

Coincidentally, I stumbled across that blog after I had face-palmed my way (sometimes literally) through a meeting in which the Ofsted Data Dashboard tables were given to governors. I couldn't quite believe that Ofsted presented the data in a way such that the average first-year physics or maths undergraduate could drive a horse and carriages right through it (if you'll excuse the Goveian metaphor). So I went home and googled the simple term 'Ofsted nonsense'. Right at the top of the list of hits were the *Icing On The Cake* posts (followed by links to many other illuminating analyses of Ofsted's assessment practices).

I'm not going to rehash those posts here – if you've got even a passing interest in the education system in England you should read them (and the associated comments threads) for yourself and reach your own conclusions. To summarise, the problems are multi-faceted but can generally be traced to simple 'rookie' flaws in data analysis. These include:

1. Inadequate appreciation of the effects of small sample size;
2. A lack of consideration of statistical significance/uncertainties in the data. (Or, at best, major deficiencies in communicating and highlighting those uncertainties);
3. Comparison of variations between schools when the variation within a given school (from year to year) can be just as large;
4. An entirely misleading placement of schools in 'quintiles' when the difference between the upper and lower quintiles can be marginal. Ofsted has already had to admit to a major flaw in its initial assignment of quintiles. [9]

What is perhaps most galling is that many A-level students in English schools will be taught to recognise and avoid these types of pitfall in data analysis. It is an irony too far that those teaching the correct approach to statistics in English classrooms are assessed and compared to their peers on the basis of Ofsted's pseudostatistical nonsense.

Philip Moriarty regularly blogs at www.muircheast.wordpress.com. This article was first published at http://physicsfocus.org/lies-damned-lies-ofsteds-pseudostatistics/

Notes:

1. http://www.theguardian.com/politics/2014/jul/15/cameron-sacks-toxic-gove-promotes-women-reshuffle
2. http://www.dailymail.co.uk/debate/article-2696687/RICHARD-LITTLEJOHN-Give-toxic-minister-dopey-headmistress.html
3. http://www.theguardian.com/politics/2014/jun/10/gove-michael-wilshaw-playground-spat
4. https://www.gov.uk/government/uploads/system/uploads/attachment_data/file/270398/Governors-Handbook-January-2014.pdf
5. http://www.telegraph.co.uk/education/10701613/Ofsted-inspections-youd-be-better-off-flipping-a-coin.html
6. http://www.policyexchange.org.uk/images/publications/watching%20the%20watchmen.pdf
7. https://www.tes.com/article.aspx?storycode=6356566
8. http://icingonthecakeblog.weebly.com/
9. http://www.naht.org.uk/welcome/news-and-media/key-topics/inspections-and-accountability/flawed-data-in-ofsted-dashboard/

Eyewitness in the classroom

Sam Keely

Starting in 2008, my five years as a student at Djanogly City Academy – an inner-city school located in a diverse and deprived area of Nottingham – raises various issues. What was it like to grow up 'in the closet' amongst a peer group dominated by casual homophobia and a pervasive sense of machismo? How was my school life – and that of my peers – affected by endemic poverty in the local community? These are all interesting avenues to explore, but much has been written on them already. This piece therefore focuses specifically on my experience of being educated in an 'academy'. When I enrolled, Djanogly City Academy was one of only a handful of academies across the country. It was a pioneer in many of the practices now common throughout the education system -- the employment of unqualified teachers, not recognising teaching unions, and the involvement of businesspeople in school governance, often to the exclusion of parents and community representatives. This makes Djanogly City Academy an interesting case to explore.

Whilst what I write is rooted in my personal experiences (and I am not claiming they are typical), I also want to reflect on the wider 'academy' debate. Within this debate, little attention has been given to the experiences of students educated at academies, and I hope to address this gap to some extent.

Much of what I say is critical of my time at Djanogly City Academy. It is therefore important to state that I genuinely enjoyed my time at school. As an un-athletic, gay 'nerd', my time there was far more positive than might have been expected. I was lucky to make friends I am still close to, and to be taught by teachers devoted to improving the lives of their students. Many teachers went well beyond what was expected of them, working through weekends, holidays and evenings to try and do the best for their students. The school's pastoral care department was particularly impressive, dealing daily with situations unthinkable in many other schools.

When Djanogly City Academy was established, in 2003, it aimed to be different from other schools. The school building expresses this aspiration perfectly. Eight thousand square metres of glass and chrome, it is singularly at odds with its surroundings, nested amongst red brick semi-detached family homes and Gothic Revival office buildings. This incongruent setting is much more than an error of architectural judgement on its designers' part. Rather, it is a statement of modernising intent: Djanogly City Academy aimed to bring education into the twenty-first century.

In my early years at the school, this ambition was pursued with zeal. Integral to it was Djanogly City Academy's status as an information technology (IT) specialist. Through its high-profile partnerships with technology companies, as well as through the business contacts of its sponsors, the school brought laptops into almost every classroom.

The ubiquitous presence of technology was key to the school's 'innovative' approach to its curriculum. As an academy, Djanogly was independent of Nottingham's Local Education Authority, as had been its predecessor, Djanogly City Technology College, which opened in 1989. It was therefore able to design its own curriculum for Key Stage Three students, and drew heavily on an educational approach called 'New Basics'. Developed in the early 2000s, 'New Basics' rejected traditional approaches towards the curriculum in favour of student-led trans-disciplinary learning, with a particular stress on Information Technology. Before it was implemented in Djanogly City Academy in 2006, the 'New Basics' approach had been used in schools in Queensland, Australia.

The influence of the 'New Basics' approach on Djanogly City Academy's curriculum was clear. Year groups were divided into 'pods', which were each assigned a small group of teachers. Rather than these teachers teaching subjects, each term centred on a particular topic – 'the Built Environment', 'Science and Ethics', 'British National Identity', and so on. Acquiring subject-specific knowledge and skills was thought to be implicit within this project-based work.

Of course, innovation in education is important. And the school's attempts to improve IT skills were welcome, especially in the early years when it could not be taken for granted that students had computers in their homes. But the new curriculum was also a manifest failure. As the senior management focused on 'New Basics', the old basics were neglected. The use of IT became overly dominant; a large number of lessons involved students making Power-Point presentations. There was pervasive boredom and disengagement in many classrooms. Many students, fearing that they were falling behind, tried to teach themselves using untouched textbooks found in classrooms. Many more, frustrated by lessons that completely failed to connect to them, became disruptive or aggressive. In itself, this is not unusual. Many secondary school students are bored and disruptive. But it was particularly acute at Djanogly City Academy. Supply teachers covering 'pod' lessons often complained that students at the school were among the least focused they had ever taught.

What was remarkable about the curriculum was how aware students were of its inadequacy. Indeed, students regularly sought to challenge it. Our sense of anger became particularly potent after the 'pod' scheme was expanded from Year Seven to the whole of Key Stage Three. I remember a close friend learning that a local news team would be on site and organising an impromptu protest. At half an hour's notice, she assembled a group of friends and attempted to march in front of the cameras with homemade signs, chanting 'Pods aren't interesting; we don't learn anything'. Similarly, when I drafted a letter to the Principal demanding more traditional lessons, it got over a hundred signatories with little effort on my part.

Such anger was understandable. It was only towards the end of our first year, and under huge student pressure, that we were taught maths. From Year Eight – the second year in the academy – onwards, we were also taught specific Science, English and IT lessons. But it was only when we began our General Certificate in Secondary Education (GCSE) studies that we were given an opportunity to study a wider range of subjects. The effect was hugely damaging; students were expected to choose GCSE options without any real understanding of what the subjects involved. Much to the irritation of our teachers, we began our GCSEs with no prior experience in the subject. I took my first German class without ever having any extended foreign language lessons before; when I began my history GCSE, I had not so much as looked at a primary source. We therefore began our GCSEs far behind many of our peers in other schools. It is a credit to the commitment of our teachers that so many of us were able to advance so far and a discredit to those who imposed the 'New Basics' curriculum that so many more did not.

It is hard to explore why the 'New Basics' curriculum was such a failure. The theory itself makes various assumptions – about levels of student engagement, the changing nature of the economy, and the rise of the 'telematic age' – and it is not at all easy to penetrate. In the particular case of Djanogly City Academy, I think the curriculum's key fault was that it suggested that the main purpose of education was to prepare students for employment. An Assistant Principal at the school argued that the curriculum was designed to teach students the 'essential practices … [needed] if they are to flourish in new times'.[1]

In effect, what was happening was a response to an economy increasingly dominated by the service sector and precarious employment. Traditional education, this approach suggested, was ineffectual in teaching students the skills they would need for life in the new economy. But these skills were too often about inculcating an 'entrepreneurial' value set in students, rather than in nurturing active and engaged learners. During 'pod' lessons, teachers would often speak about the 'business world' that we were all expected to enter one day. It is not surprising that it failed to engage or inspire students.

And yet, despite these 'modernising' aspirations, the school was underpinned by essentially conservative principles. The practice of wealthy benefactors 'sponsoring' (although not funding) local academies is rooted in the voluntaristic mindset of the Victorian era, which saw a resurgence with Cameron's 'Big Society'. These ideals were clearly embodied in the school's annual Founders' Evening. Ostensibly about rewarding the achievements of the school's pupils, the evening was an opportunity for businesses and wealthy entrepreneurs to demonstrate their moral rectitude by donating the prizes that would be won by students. Deference was a strong theme on these occasions. Teachers and students had to stand and applaud as these 'founders' entered the room, and students – including me, one year – were made to deliver speeches thanking them for their contributions to the school. However, much of this was illusory; the relationship between these so-called 'founders' and the school at any other time of the year was marginal, and whilst we were all told to value their generosity, the school was actually mostly publicly funded.

But what about the teachers? Teachers' attitudes always affect their students, and throughout my time at the school, I was conscious of a deep discontent amongst many of the teachers there. This showed itself in a very high turnover rate. Teachers often left halfway through a year, with many of them finding jobs outside of education.

Management's relationship with staff seemed to have played a major part in creating these feelings. For many years, senior management exploited the school's status as a 'new build' academy to deny recognition to teaching unions. This restricted teachers' sense of professional competence, despite 'New Basics' supposedly enhancing their autonomy. Management could therefore act with relative impunity. This created a prevailing sense of fear amongst the teaching staff. Teachers would privately admit serious misgivings about the direction the school was taking, but there was little they could do about it without union recognition. And whilst many teachers spoke to me about their concerns, they insisted that I be discreet for fear of reprisals from management.

Even when unions were eventually recognised, the management continued to treat staff with distrust. A striking fact about the design of the school's buildings was that there was no single staffroom that all teachers could use. Instead, teachers were allocated small staff rooms on a departmental basis. This division limited their capacity to communicate and organise. The teachers' confidence was not helped by the widespread use of short-term contracts, and the consequent anxiety many felt.

Teachers' professionalism was also undermined by the high number of unqualified staff employed by the school. By 2013, unqualified teachers constituted one-fifth of the whole teaching staff, with deleterious effects on students' lives, including mine. I was taught by many unqualified teachers. While many of them had a great understanding of their subject, their experience of teaching young people was minimal. Many struggled to manage their classes and to get their knowledge across. This meant that their qualified colleagues often had to oversee classes to keep lessons on track, taking them away from their own classrooms.

The employment of unqualified teachers did not only involve staff without basic teaching qualifications. Many lessons were taught by trained teachers with no experience in those subjects. The second year of my sociology GCSE was taught first by my former history teacher, and later by a design and technology teacher. I liked them both, but neither was qualified to teach sociology. With little subject knowledge, both tried to teach from 'life experience'. It was only two weeks before the exam that we were taught by a trained sociology teacher. This had a devastating effect: many students who worked hard to get good grades in the first year, failed to get 'C' grades by the end.

Why did the school have so many problems? There is no simple answer here. Any school in a community with such high levels of deprivation will face challenges that other schools do not. It seems to me, however, that a fundamental issue was the inability of senior management to really understand the local area. Few, if any, of the school's headteachers lived locally, and their attitudes and assumptions seemed out of touch with the needs and expectations of the local community. This is clearly illustrated by the fact that the school was originally intended to be partially selective. This would have deprived many young people in the area of a local school. It was only due to the intervention of community activists – my late grandmother amongst them – that the Academy agreed to drop its plans and guarantee places for local children.

But the senior management of the Djanogly City Academy also had unrealistic expectations, which were expressed throughout my time at the school. I recall my last headteacher proclaiming that he would make the school one of the highest achieving in the city. Whilst all headteachers should aspire to the best for their pupils, this ambition, I felt, was a matter of rhetoric rather than reality. Half of Djanogly City Academy's students spoke English as a second language, 54% were supported by Pupil Premium – a fund intended to close the attainment gap between disadvantaged children and their peers – and the number of students with special educational needs was three times higher than the national average.

There was potential for massive improvements in Djanogly City Academy; it could easily have been capable of effecting positive change in the lives of many young people. But it would never top the league tables based on its results. And it shouldn't have been expected to. Rather than focusing on league tables, senior management should have treated students as individuals, and worked, as ordinary teachers did, on having a positive effect on their lives. Unfortunately, senior management seemed more interested in attainment than achievement. Students suffered as a result. In my year, hundreds were not given the opportunity to sit GCSEs but sat BTECs – school leaving qualifications designed by the Business and Technology Education Council – instead, to improve the school's statistics.

Behaviour was another area where the failings of senior management became clear. As noted earlier, disruptive behaviour was a frequent problem at Djanogly City Academy. During my time at the school, increasingly severe countermeasures were introduced to combat poor behaviour – an isolation area, a high number of exclusions, even the school's own off-site Pupil Referral Unit. But none were particularly effective. On one occasion, the school even made local headlines when it sent 56 pupils home for wearing the wrong shoes. However, disruption continued to be a significant problem and exclusions remained high, because many of the key issues which caused poor behaviour – disengagement with education, emotional problems, a sense of pessimism about the future – were not dealt with.

Notes

1. S. Sharma, 'Education: a revolutionary process @ Djanogly City Academy', *Association for Learning Technology*. Accessible at <http://archive.alt.ac.uk/alt.newsweaver.co.uk/newsweaver.co.uk/alt/e article00092493564.html?=b11.0.w> [Accessed 27th June, 2016].

9

Making space for asking questions

Kiri Tunks

How effective is social media in facilitating active political citizenship?

What significance do languages hold in people's lives and does it matter if we lose them?

Is conflict inevitable and is it ever possible to resolve it?

These are three questions that students in my school have been attempting to answer as part of their exam coursework for something called 'Global Perspectives' (GP). Cambridge International Examinations run the course as an 'iGCSE' and a 'Pre-U' (pre-university) alternative to GCSE (general certificate of secondary education) and A-Level examinations. It is a course of study you are more likely to find in private schools as an extra qualification for students aiming for university.

But last year my school, a fully inclusive comprehensive in East London, made the decision that we would deliver Global Perspectives to all students in key stage three (KS3) for one lesson a week and offer it at key stage four and key stage five as an exam course. The course is a mixture of critical thinking, current affairs and investigative research. On one level, it fills a gap left by citizenship and personal, social and health education (PSHE), but it also crosses over with other subjects such as the humanities, English, science and technology. Unlike many of those other subjects, the Global Perspectives curriculum offers students a lot of choice about what they study and demands an independence that can be sorely lacking in the rigid, content-based curriculum generally imposed on schools.

The catch for the school is that the Global Perspectives exam doesn't carry any points for 'Progress 8' – the new benchmark for school performance – and isn't an A-Level. My school has made space for it because we are conscious that the current curriculum isn't providing the breadth of knowledge and understanding about the world our young people now live in. We also know that years of being taught to the test is leaving young people poorly prepared for the independent academic world of university and for life beyond academia.

Another factor in introducing Global Perspectives was undoubtedly as a response to the 'Prevent' agenda – the British government's controversial 'anti-extremism strategy'. Our students are mainly from the Bengali Muslim community and they would be considered by the government to be at risk of 'radicalisation'. After the incident when three girls from Bethnal Green went to Syria, there could have been a temptation to shut down debate and try to close out the world. My school's response was more sophisticated and we created the department of Global Perspectives to bring the world in. The school decided that the best way to 'prevent' our young people from making dangerous choices was to openly discuss the issues and to create safe spaces where they could debate ideas and events whilst being taught to apply strong critical thinking skills.

The Global Perspectives approach has resulted in some fabulous work, some moments of genuine revelation for everyone, and the development of some very switched-on young people. It has also enabled us to talk about 'British' values in a serious and analytical way. If these values are to mean anything then they must be upheld in practice.

The course is global in many ways – the world and its people are our primary study resource and our questions are universal ones that can be applied to any country. We have been able to focus on hidden or underrepresented places. We have been able to go off at tangents and respond to world events. For example, in 2015 Syria featured in conversations a lot. Our Year 10 students then took part in a project with the United Nations Work and Relief Agency (UNWRA) funded by the European Union and the Department for International Development in which they collaborated with refugee children in Damascus. Initially, we were nervous about taking part, worried how it would be represented in the media and elsewhere. But in the end, the school realised it would be hypocritical to turn down the project when we would have agreed to it with any other country.

The project has proved to be truly inspirational. Our students have video-called students in Syria and both groups talked about their lives and their ideas for a high quality education. In just three calls, the friendship they felt and the education they underwent was really something to see. The real-time, real-life connection with young people living in very different circumstances was mind changing. Our students were utterly inspired by the young Damascans, their commitment to learning, and their determined aspiration. It taught us all a little something about resilience.

All this was happening at the time of a conference in London to increase aid for Syria and we were caught up in a media flurry. So, as well as the project itself, our young people found themselves interviewed by London Live and CNN, featured in the *Evening Standard*, other local press and several online news sites. A group of them were invited to interview Justine Greening MP, Minister for International Development, for BBC School Report and this was shown on BBC London News.

One of the things that Global Perspectives students need to do as part of their group work is produce an outcome related to their research. At the end of the project, as well as all the media work publicising the plight of children in Syria, the students had written to Philip Hammond MP, Secretary of State at the Foreign and Commonwealth Office, asking the government to do more. Students also gave assemblies about the project to other year groups, and organised a fundraising week for UNWRA, making cakes, collecting coppers and small change, and lobbying for a non-uniform day. They raised hundreds of pounds.

This Syria project is a bit out of the ordinary and doesn't represent routine delivery of the course. But having Global Perspectives on the curriculum meant we were able to accommodate the opportunity when it came. We had the flexibility to respond and adapt. It was brilliant to be able to react to a current news story and model for our young people ways of making contact and working with others, as well as them being active agents in trying to bring about change. They have learnt to work in a group and coordinate action. They've learnt that to advocate something, you need to be informed. They've also learnt that they have the right to ask questions and expect properly formulated answers. But it is clear that, despite the obvious positive impact, this kind of work in schools is uncommon or, at least, only managed in spite of the current restrictive curriculum and high stakes testing agenda, both of which are huge obstacles to such exciting and very real learning. This work happens in pockets, but it will be where schools have the confidence and a good Ofsted (Office for Standards in Education) grading. It will mostly be an add-on, not at the heart of the learning process.

Some of what is taught in Global Perspectives can't be tested in a standard exam. It's largely coursework, and some of that is done as a group project. Yet the course is hugely popular with students and highly valued because it creates a space to discuss issues they don't get to discuss anywhere else. It gives them the skills to question and challenge what they hear; and it allows students to develop expertise on global issues and concepts. As one student puts it:

> *'Global Perspectives has taught me to be more sceptical about news stories and it challenges your critical thinking skills. This has enabled me to make better judgements of local/national and international issues.'*
> *Miriam*

This is a powerful thing. Students very quickly start to realise that learning isn't just about seeking the correct answer but about being able to ask the right questions. As Thomas Pynchon says in *Gravity's Rainbow*:

> *'If they can get you asking the wrong questions, they don't have to worry about the answers.'*

Asking good questions is very empowering: it exposes hype and bluster; it reveals lies and prejudice; it helps you find better answers.

In key stage three, we've been able to create a curriculum that suits the different years and groups. One focus has been on 'Global Products'. Year 7 students learn about the origins and production of chocolate; in Year 8 the focus is on chewing gum; in Year 9 it's on the mobile phone.

The idea of looking at global products is to reflect on what the products mean to us: what their positive and negative impacts are;

and the implications of their production. So, through a chocolate tasting session, Year 7 students came to understand how different percentages of cocoa affects the taste and price of a bar. By role-playing the trading of cocoa beans, they learnt how the chocolate trade affects producers and consumers.

The mobile phone unit allowed us to discuss the pros and cons of mobile phone use, but also those of production, particularly in relation to mining coltan – a metallic ore used in electronic devices – in places such as the Democratic Republic of Congo. This unit gave us the space to improve knowledge about Africa generally so that students stopped referring to it as a 'country' and realised Africa is actually a continent comprising 54 very different countries. They also learnt that Africa is becoming known as the 'mobile continent' as people there have taken up mobile phone technology in increasingly innovative ways. This increased knowledge about an under-taught area of the world, and also challenged stereotypes of what it means to be 'African'.

We also encourage our students to develop argumentation skills. Year 7 students have to pick a really stupid idea and then argue in favour of it. This task implicitly requires them to look at something from a different angle and, for example, they love coming up with reasons why we should all live in houses made of jelly, or play soccer with a fiery football! Of course, the process of arguing for such ideas inevitably led them to rationalise why these ideas are 'stupid', but we also asked them to modify the idea and see if they could take something positive from it. This led to ideas about making houses less angular and more colourful, and an understanding of the importance of safety at public sporting events.

Topics such as global inequality and feminism also work well. The students have really impressed us with their ability to reflect and adjust opinions and challenge their own prejudices, whether tackling domestic violence, abusive language, or the qualities of a leader. Perhaps most impressive was the response of Year 8 boys after we gave only the girls a chocolate at the start of the lesson as a way of modelling inequality. After the initial cries of 'it's not fair', all the students threw themselves into the activities about how women's inequality manifests itself across the world. At the end of the lesson, some of the boys asked if they could have their chocolate now. When we said 'no, that's not how the world works,' they smiled and accepted the lesson with good grace.

Year 9 have been fascinated by the project on prisons in which we compare the UK system to those in other countries, look at youth offending, issues of race and gender, and debated whether prisoners should have the right to vote. Many students shifted their starting point of 'lock them up and throw away the key' when faced with the evidence of how many prisons are failing to treat people equally or fairly, keep people safe, or prevent re-offending.

In the current year, we have been planning pretty much as we go. Although this has been tricky at times, it has enabled us to be quite organic in our approach. We are able to pick topics that are current, or respond to the interests and needs of students. This has meant that when we teach, the students are generally engaged and motivated.

One of the best things about Global Perspectives is not the increasing knowledge about global affairs and different countries; it's not even the increased scepticism and critical thinking skills; it's the insight and reflection it has given us on own lives and our own experiences. I say 'our' because this course really is one where learning is part of the teachers' experience too. We have all got better at realising how much we have in common with people who live somewhere else, as well as how much we have to learn from their lives and their opinions. Even where we disagree, students are learning to respect such difference as a way of strengthening their own understanding.

The independent research question 'what is belief and does it unite or divide us?' led one student to interview the local Anglican parish priest, an atheist teacher and a Catholic student, as well as reflecting on how different members of her own Muslim family practise their beliefs differently.

The question of minority languages led another student to compare the loss of the Andamanese 'Bo' language with the concerted revival of Maori through the establishment of *Te Reo Māori* schools in New Zealand. But beyond this, the most profound discovery was how important Bengali was to her own mother, who had lived through the 1971 Bengali War of Independence and the struggles people fought to have the right to speak it. This was a topic they had never spoken about before. It led the student to realise how little she had valued her family language and had, instead, prioritised speaking English.

> *'Overall, I feel as if my opinion towards language has changed, and in the process of exploring different cultures as well as my own, I have been made to think deeply about what it would mean if the Bengali language would not be remembered by a generation that would come 50 years from now. I feel that it would mean that wars that were fought and the suffering it took to even establish a Bengali culture would have been done in vain.'*
>
> *Rahima*

Overall, the value and importance of creating spaces in school for the individual and collective interrogation of big global questions has created a healthy respect for difference of experience and thought.

> *'There's no right or wrong answer to things: everyone speaks their opinion.'*
>
> *Suraya*

And students continue to surprise and be surprised – when your most fervent feminist is wearing a hijab and arguing for a woman's right to wear whatever she wants without being harassed; when the boys are calling others out on sexism; or when a teenage Christian girl slams the demonisation of Islam, you know you are in a really interesting space. This has to be better than a situation where young people do not speak out in case their names are put on a register.

10

How social control
dresses up as social justice

Mary Compton

'I think the aim should be for everyone across the world … to understand what we mean by education … and if I am a parent what kind of education I would like for my child – an education which makes all children independent thinkers, independent learners, being able to think and critically engage … If it is not then I'm sorry – I think we should not go for it – we should not even think about it.' (Education activist in Mumbai)

In a corrugated iron shed with holes for windows, a young teacher stands at a shabby blackboard reading from a scripted arithmetic lesson. As he calls out questions, the children in front of him chant out answers with more or less enthusiasm or apparent understanding. Through the gap where the door should be, we can hear a continual cacophony of shouting and talking. It must be very hot under the tin, but the teacher and children soldier on, no doubt conscious of the video camera filming them for a 'Sample Teaching Video' for Bridge International Academies' 'low fee' private school chain in Kenya.

In schools all over the global South, both public and private, teachers are struggling to teach and children to learn in conditions like these, hard for those of us who teach in the North to imagine. Some learning takes place under trees, because there are no classrooms available – even in ostensibly successful economies like South Africa. Thousands of schools have no sanitation. Books are scarce. Many schools have no furniture. Class sizes are frequently well over a hundred to one teacher. Teachers' pay can be as little as $1 a day and often is not a lot more. Many teachers and children are working in situations where they have no protection from violence – for example in North East Kenya where Boko Haram operate, or Yemen where schools are targeted by Saudi air raids.

Recently there was justified outrage in the United States about the appalling conditions in Detroit public schools, where vermin infestations and holes in the roof are not uncommon as well as failing air conditioning and heating systems. Just as in the global South, the majority of children attending these schools are children of colour from low income families. In the words of the education activist quoted above – neither the conditions in Detroit nor those in the global South are 'the kind of education I would like for my child'. Indeed it is a miracle that education goes on at all in many schools – in some cases it is even a miracle that teachers are able to survive.

Just as in Detroit, where a caucus inside the teachers union organised a 'sick-out' to draw attention to the conditions, teachers in the global South, usually organised into unions, are fighting for public education: demanding safe and decent learning conditions, pay which will allow them to escape from poverty, and enough trained teachers to enable reasonable class sizes. The nature of that fightback varies from country to country, but it usually takes the form of strikes, sometimes indefinite, as well as street protests and occupations. Frequently, school students demonstrate in support of their teachers, blaming governments rather than unions for the failure to come up with the funding for their education. Often teachers and their students are met with violent police retaliation. In India, it is common to see teachers being beaten by the police with lathis (long sticks). In other places, for instance in Brazil, more high tech oppression is used – tear gas and water canon. Teachers are frequently arrested and, in some cases such as Bahrain and Iran, imprisoned and even tortured or executed. These often heroic struggles of teachers for public education are routinely ignored by the world's media. Instead, and in so far as they are interested in educational justice, they focus on the efforts of international organisations and their celebrity cheerleaders.

For international capital and its spokesperson the World Bank, the situation in which millions of children are out of school or in schools which are grossly inadequate is impossible to ignore. Indeed if capitalism is to have any chance of continuing to grow its profits, it is vital to have at least minimally educated global workers and consumers. For that reason 'Education for All' has become one of the leading professed goals of the World Bank in its mission to 'end poverty'. It is also high on the agenda of the elites who gather at the

World Economic Forum in Davos to 'improve the state of the world.'

It would seem self-evident that the first thing necessary for any kind of campaign to get children into school and learning would be to ensure adequate infrastructure, resources and safety, as well as decently paid, qualified and trained teachers. All these things cost a great deal of money. However, in document after document, the World Bank makes clear that it is not primarily a lack of funding which causes educational injustice. No, the most important break on the development of 'Education for All' is the failure of teachers and the interference of their unions. What is important, according to this narrative, is not adequate funding but 'great' teaching. So, for example, the major World Bank policy document *Making Schools Work* has a picture on the front of a global South teacher with his feet up on his desk asleep. The text starts from the premise: 'this book is about the threats to education quality that cannot be explained by lack of resources'. Or in the more recent document, *Great Teachers*, the author says: 'all of the available evidence suggests that the quality of Latin American and Caribbean teachers is the binding constraint on the region's progress towards world class education systems'. Similarly, the biggest education corporation, Pearson, asserts: 'teacher quality is widely regarded as the school-related factor that has the biggest impact on student achievement, far more than books, facilities or curriculum'.

No one, least of all teachers, would want to underestimate the transformative difference that they can make. But very few teachers could make a difference without the basic conditions in which living, learning and teaching are possible. So why is this not taken as the first job in any campaign to bring about 'Education for All'? The obvious answer would be that it is much easier to blame teachers than to provide the level of aid needed to solve the immediate problems described above. However, aid is itself a contested issue, more often than not tied to conditions which undermine local democracy and favour the interests of donor countries. What teachers globally are fighting for is not more aid from rich countries, but for their own governments to provide adequate resources. So why is that not happening? Many countries in the global South have very restricted budgets largely because they are paying out infinitely more to the rich North than they receive in aid, both in debt repayments, and in the pillaging of their resources together with the concomitant tax avoidance of large corporations. In Kenya alone, for example, it is calculated that $6 billion a year is lost through tax avoidance by foreign corporations. In Malawi it has recently come to light that UK corporations, the third biggest investors in the country, are paying no tax to the government on the basis of a 60-year-old treaty. Add to that the fact that the local political classes are often bought off by the same corporations and send their own children to elite private schools and you have a great deal of the explanation for the failure to fund schools properly.

The World Bank facilitates much of the 'ease of doing business' which makes corporate resource pillaging and tax avoidance possible, so it is unlikely to criticise those practices in order to free up funds for education. Blaming teachers is therefore a convenient starting point. However, there is more to it than that. By framing the need to 'improve' teachers and schools in social justice terms, a space is opened up for significant profits for education corporations to provide the machinery of accountability and choice: standardised testing and curricula, data collection, teacher evaluation and privatisation, in short the whole framework which is so depressingly familiar to those of us who teach in the North and which has become known as the Global Education Reform Movement or GERM.

It almost defies belief that in a country like Pakistan where teachers face all the problems caused by lack of funding, as well as in parts of the country threats to life and limb from endemic violence, performance related pay is being introduced. Largely responsible for this are Pearson and the UK Department for International Development, which paid that company's chief education adviser to 'reform' the education system in the Punjab region of the country. Needless to say, performance related pay is being fought by teachers with the same determination as they are fighting for permanent contracts, decent conditions and a living wage. Nor is Pakistan the only country where this is happening. It is spreading across the global South like the GERM it is – most recently to Kenya in the wake of a long and as yet unresolved teachers' strike for a living wage.

So for the World Bank and its client corporations GERM provides a win-win situation – there is no need for extra tax to be paid or to stop pillaging, and in providing 'quality' education you can also make lots of money. In fact there is a third win – the GERM tools also allow capital to dictate the kind of education which is and indeed is not given – it destroys teacher autonomy and potentially controls the curriculum.

Co-opting the curriculum

When the National Curriculum was introduced in the United Kingdom by the Thatcher Government in the 1980s, it was contested by those who saw such a development as a step towards totalitarianism. One leading educationist described hearing the 'distant march of jackboots'. Such opposition has largely disappeared, even in the teaching unions themselves. Only when some new outrage is committed by right wing education secretaries such as the removal of non-English literature from the syllabus, or excessive tampering with the history syllabus, does the inherent danger of allowing a state to dictate what is taught become obvious.

Equally worrying is the idea that the curriculum should be dictated by a corporation – and not just for its own country but for schools all over the world. Yet that is exactly what is happening. Firms like Pearson are developing teaching materials and standardised testing to go with them and selling them to sovereign governments or franchising them out to private school chains. It is what they call in a promotional video, 'uncoupling lesson design from lesson delivery'. What this means translated from management speak is clear from the video: every word the teacher utters is written down in a 21 page script for a 35 minute lesson. More often than not, these materials are in English, which for many countries in the global South is regarded as the language of aspiration and success. This is very convenient for corporations since it is much easier to produce standardised materials in English than in the thousands of languages which are the birthright of the world's children. But even more importantly, scripting lessons allows them to produce materials which suit the needs of capital – ensuring if possible that children have basic skills such as literacy and numeracy, but giving teachers no freedom to learn with children about the world they live in and ask questions, for example, about the economic relations which lead to the poverty in which most find themselves.

Let us go back to the Indian activist quoted at the beginning of this chapter. She says she would want her child to be able to 'think and critically engage with (the world)'. She is a member of an Indian group which is bringing critical education into Mumbai public schools by working with teachers and providing them with materials and training. In this work they are attempting to supplant the deadening legacy of rote-learning left by India's old colonial masters, with the more enlightened educational methodology of some indigenous Indian educators. All over the world, activists, teachers and their unions are engaged in similar struggles. In Peru, for example, the teachers union is developing courses using the methods of Lev Vygotsky and Paolo Freire in order to reach distant peasant communities. In Mexico, where some of the sharpest struggles are taking place, the dissident teachers' faction CNTE in the Oaxaca region, working with local communities, has developed its own curriculum and collaborative evaluation methods, based on local indigenous languages and culture. In Pakistan and in Spain teachers have fought against the imposition of English and the downgrading or even punishing of local languages.

The attempt to introduce a national curriculum in the US, known as the Common Core, has also been dressed up in the language of social justice. The Common Core, so the argument goes, will see the child in Louisiana having the same chances as the child in Seattle, since they will all be learning the same thing. This move has excited much more opposition than it has in the UK, both from the libertarian right and from the left. Tea Party radicals see it as the encroachment of the federal state on decisions which should be made locally. Educationists on the left see it as an attack on professional autonomy and the freedom to teach creatively and critically. However, the leaderships of the two teaching unions, the American Federation of Teachers (AFT) and the National Education Association (NEA), have been enthusiastic supporters of the Common Core and indeed have taken money from the Gates Foundation to help develop it.

As I have described above, just like the US government and the foundations and corporations pushing the Common Core, the World Bank and its clients use the language of social justice to promote their interests. It is this which creates a space for teachers' own organisations to co-operate with organisations such as the World Bank and the Gates Foundation. For example, the Global Partnership for Education, supported by the World Bank, has Education International, the federation of teaching unions and associations, as one of its members, as does the Universal Learning Metrics Taskforce, which is jointly convened by the UNESCO Institute of Statistics and the Center for Universal Education at the Brookings Institution. In both organisations, Pearson has a more prominent role than Education International, which merely has a seat at the table. Teaching unions too often fail to unpick the GERM rhetoric in order to understand its ideological underpinning.

It seems to me there are two dominant reactions by teachers who are rightly appalled by the injustice and inequality in educational opportunities around the world. One is what you might call the 'Bandaid' reaction. You get your school, for example, to sponsor a school in Kenya and raise money for pens and teaching materials or even new buildings. At the same time you teach your children to 'think globally' and empathetically about children in the rest of the world (but risk reinforcing the perception of global South children as passive, if deserving victims with no agency in their own lives). The other reaction is through lobbying the very organisations which are largely responsible for the injustice. For example, you get children to send letters to the UK Prime Minister asking him to increase aid to Africa, fostering the illusion that people such as Gordon Brown or David Cameron are either able or willing to solve the inequality which so damages our world. Or if you are a global union federation, you sit on the Universal Learning Metrics Taskforce (whose co-chair, incidentally, is the same Sir Michael Barber mentioned above) and attempt to influence it towards more benign policies towards teaching unions and teachers. I have no doubt that all of these actions are well meaning, motivated by a real desire to make the world a better place for teachers and children. However, in co-operating with the World Bank and its institutions we risk giving credibility to its false rhetoric of social justice, which is being used to attack democratic education, teachers and children all over the world.

Perhaps the reason so many teachers opt for the Bandaid root and union leaders opt for collaboration with international financial institutions is that the problem seems so vast. How can you train and pay all those teachers, build all those schools, provide all those resources? I would frame the question from the opposite standpoint, however. How can you not? Remember the question – 'is this the education I would like for my child?' and if it's not good enough for a child in Bristol, Berlin or Boston, why should it be for a child in Delhi, Dhaka or Dar es Salaam?

We in the North have got much to learn from the struggles of teachers in the South. Not only from the determination and often heroism of their struggles for education funding and against GERM policies, but also from the understanding many of them show of the need to defend education and schools as democratic spaces. The idea that the curriculum should be based on local cultures, languages and histories in a collaboration between teachers and communities has been largely missing from our discourse, particularly in the UK, although interestingly it is the way the curriculum is developed in Finland, one of the poster countries for educational excellence.

Social justice is what the majority of readers of this book are engaged in promoting and fighting for. Yet we are allowing it to be used as a disguise by the very organisations which promote injustice and inequality. They are using it to cover up their push for profits and social control of the children of the world. If we truly believe in the struggle for the schools our children deserve, then children in the global South are just as deserving as those in the North. We must insist that our unions see through the social justice disguise of the GERM merchants, learn from our colleagues in the South, and fight for 'the kind of school I would like for my child … all across the world'.

All of the stories mentioned in this chapter can be read on the website www.teachersolidarity.com

11

We are the penicillin to the GERM!

Kristine Mayle

Kristine Mayle is the Treasurer of the Chicago Teachers Union. What follows is her address to the 2015 conference of the National Union of Teachers in Harrogate.

… I am excited to be back speaking with my sisters and brothers of the NUT. I've watched in excitement your various work actions last year, cheered along with you when Michael Gove finally got gone, and the Chicago Teachers Union and its members have been following the Stand Up for Education campaign and watching how parents and community have sympathized with teachers and their 60-hour work weeks.

I'm here with two simple messages to you. Firstly, you are not alone. Secondly, there are ways to fight back and win. I had the pleasure of participating last spring in a wonderful conference hosted by the NUT where educators from all over the world came to discuss the Global Education Reform Movement, the GERM. We heard about the ways that public education is being destroyed by business interests in a calculated, coordinated way. The same types of initiatives I see in Chicago and across the United States are the exact same ones being used in Asia, Africa, South and Central America, and of course here in the UK and in other parts of Europe. The attacks on our students and teachers take different forms in different places, with mutations to make the GERM more effective depending on where it is active. For example, in India, the GERM takes advantage of the caste system and all that encompasses. In Mexico, it uses corrupt police and government officials to disappear student teachers that stand up for public education. In the United States, it attacks where communities are already weakened. New Orleans' entire school system was privatised immediately after Hurricane Katrina and the Secretary of Education, Arne Duncan, called it 'the best thing to happen to public education in New Orleans'. Elsewhere, budget crises prompt massive school closures, cuts to teachers' pensions, and privatisation of public schools.

Looking at the Stand Up for Education pages on the NUT's website, I see many similarities between the GERM attacks on public education in the UK and back home. Your 'conversion' is our 'turnaround'. Your 'appraisals' are our teacher and school rating systems, 'Performance Evaluation Reform Act' (PERA) in my home state, which ties students' standardised test scores to teachers' performance ratings, and can lead to job loss. Your 'academies' are our 'charters'; they both mean privatisation.

Some words are surrounded by controversy in both places:

Poverty – the real cause of alleged school failure. In Chicago and many other big cities, a student's postal zip code is the best predictor of standardised test performance.

Pensions – they want to take our hard-earned retirement investments because bankers crashed the economy.

Testing – too much time on meaningless tests that don't measure anything but poverty levels (and they are used to make corporations rich).

Which leads me to Pearson. The Common Core State Standards imposed upon us by Pearson were created by non-educators, are woefully off level, discourage critical thinking and the use of context. Imagine giving a student the Magna Carta to read, but leaving out all context! That is what the Common Core State Standards do!

Workload is the number one complaint I hear from my members. They spend their days analysing data, restructuring their lesson plans, reporting on the data, inserting five grades per class per week, analysing more data. Our special education teachers are so busy testing and doing paperwork that our kids don't receive their special education services.

But there is hope. I'm here to let you know that teachers in the United States are standing up and your own union is doing the same. The quick version of what happened in Chicago goes like this. Renaissance 2010 was devised as a plan to 'transform' the Chicago Public Schools. The plan was to close 100 'failing' schools and open 100 'successful' schools in their place. They targeted schools in poverty-stricken neighbourhoods, places with a lot of public housing, and where unemployment and gang violence were the norm. Instead of putting resources into the schools (which educators know would have been the real way to improve student learning), they closed them and replaced them with quasi-public/private charters. Tens of thousands of students were displaced, thousands of teachers and school support staff lost their jobs, and what replaced them were novice, unqualified teachers who didn't know what they were doing, who were being led by people who weren't educators. And this was supposed to 'close the inequality gap!' You won't be surprised to hear it didn't work.

Neighbourhood schools are the centre of community. They hold things together, especially in neighbourhoods with nothing else. They started with five to ten schools being closed for performance, then ten to twenty for performance, under-utilisation, bad test scores, whatever they could invent as criteria. This continued for a decade.

Early in 2008, a group of teachers had had enough. We started organizing to fight back. My school, along with 15 others, was placed on the chopping block. Social justice minded teachers got together to see what could be done. We started with a book club reading *The Shock Doctrine* by Naomi Klein – if you haven't read it, you should. What we realised was that we already had the mechanism to fight back, we just weren't using it correctly. Chicago teachers belong to the Chicago Teachers Union, Local 1 of the American Federation of Teachers. It was formed in the fightbacks of the past, tracing its roots to the early 20th century.

We forced our union to look at its role and its potential power differently. We no longer wanted bread-and-butter or service unionism, we wanted members to become active, to control their own destiny. We wanted to see an end to reactive actions to things being done TO us – we wanted to change the course.

Importantly, we also saw the need to bring in other stakeholders. We were tired of 'THEM' controlling our schools and our futures. We wanted to, saw the imperative to, band 'US' together. There were more of US than THEM. We, the US, knew more about our students and communities than the THEM, and we knew that to change anything, we'd need each other.

We formed a coalition which we named GEM – The Grassroots

Education Movement. It included community groups, mostly from neighbourhoods of colour, those that had been targeted in closures. There were also parent groups, some that had been fighting virtually alone for years. There was a teacher group other than the union, a group of social justice minded teachers that emphasized empowering students through their teaching methods and curricula. Coalition work is tough, and should be. If you are truly bringing together different representative groups, those groups will at times have competing notions, different motivations, different focuses, and all those forces will pull in different directions. But if your overall goal is the same, and ours was, to protect and preserve public education in the city of Chicago, you can find ways to make it work.

The relationships, common language, friendships and solidarity that we fomented in that early coalition continue to this day. The roots of those coalitions helped the Chicago Teachers Union launch and win a successful week-and-a-half-long strike. Months before our strike, while we were organising school building by school building, our coalition partners helped guide us in the creation of our research paper, 'The Schools Chicago's Students Deserve'. Based on the priorities of our teachers, parents and community members we worked with, we developed a road map, not unlike your Stand Up for Education Manifesto. We laid out our vision of what schooling should be – fully staffed and resourced schools, arts, music, physical education for all students, wrap around services like nursing and social work for our students, especially those living in trauma. The solution to so-called failing schools wasn't to shutter them or fill them with unqualified teachers, it was to provide them with what they had been lacking for decades.

Through the report and the demands we made we won the public to our side. They saw that we weren't just fighting for teachers' salaries or pensions, but that the teachers were fighting for their children. In return, the parents and community fought for our teachers. Our message was simple – we wanted the same things for our students that the mayor's kids had. Since the message was so simple yet so broad, our members were great at articulating it. Any of our members were capable of pleading our case to parents and their neighbours with personal stories of what their schools and classrooms were lacking.

Teachers' strikes are rarely popular, but ours was. Teachers, parents and supporters rallied by their schools in the mornings, then marched downtown in the afternoons. They shut the business district down every day for nine days. Remarkably, the support did not just come from Chicago. Teachers and trade unionists from across the country parachuted into town to lend a hand. On the sixth day of our strike a poll showed that fully 60 per cent of the parents in the city still supported us – an unheard-of number!

We ended up winning a lot in our contract. Huge monetary gains for our members weren't one of those wins. But you know what? Our members didn't mind. We had won back some dignity, some pride, and some improved conditions for our students.

Most importantly, we built more lasting coalitions and found more allies. The Chicago Teachers Union is now *the* trusted voice on education issues in the city of Chicago. Parents and the media alike turn to us for guidance. Since the strike we've had testing opt-outs led by parents and teachers. Sadly, we've also been punished. The mayor closed 50 schools in a single year – and paid a political price for it. We held the first mayoral run-off election in decades. Sadly, Rahm Emmanuel won a second term as mayor of Chicago. But a ray of hope is that Susan Sadlowski Garza, a school counsellor and CTU Area Vice President and school delegate, was elected to City Council. Sue and the other 12 members of the Progressive Caucus will continue the fight in the Council and we are proud to have a union sister representing us there.

The movement has caught fire. Unions across the United States have copied our plan and expanded it. There are now documents describing the schools St. Paul's, Los Angeles', Seattle's, and Milwaukee's students deserve. Each modified and expanded to meet their particular needs. Our fightback network continues to grow and our tactics continue to evolve. It feels as though we are becoming the penicillin to the GERM. We are weakening it even though it is still fighting.

A critical yet basic union principle tells me that we will win. There are more of us than them. We are growing faster and stronger than them. Each victorious strike, each well-written student-focused manifesto makes us stronger.

Solidarity forever!

SEVERE WEATHER WARNING — STORM NICKY

#hands off our schools #tellNicky NO

12

Farewell critical friend!

Tony Simpson

When I became a local authority governor, in the early 1990s, I was asked to be a 'critical friend' to the voluntary aided primary school on whose governing body I had volunteered to serve. This was how the role was characterised. By the time I resigned, 20 years later, with 'academisation' imminent, governors were being asked to indemnify the successor multi-academy trust against losses in the future which might arise as a consequence of decisions taken by the governing body of which I had been a part. What possible losses were envisaged? Was it, for example, that a former employee might sue the trust over damage to health whilst working at the school? This was never made clear, but it seemed to me a wholly inappropriate request to make to the school's friends, critical or not.

What was changing? Principally, the legal status of the school was being transformed. Prior to 'academisation', most schools were part of the local authority, although voluntary aided ones usually collaborated closely with the local authority while the buildings (but not the land, necessarily) belonged, in most cases, to one of the churches. The church was also the employer in the case of voluntary aided schools.

The overwhelming majority of schools, often described as 'community schools', were 'maintained' as part of the local education authority. Their land, buildings, fixtures and fittings, equipment and books belonged to the local authority, which was also the employer of teachers and support staff.

All this changes with so-called 'academisation', a legal process that incorporates schools as 'private limited companies by guarantee without share capital'. This makes the schools legal persons in their own right. There are no 'shares' in company schools, but the 'members' of the trust which owns the school pledge to pay a small amount (often £10) in the event that the company fails. (Have such guarantees been honoured when academy company schools have failed?)

Company schools can be sued as legal persons in their own right. They are subject to the full range of law and litigation within which trading companies operate. So, for example, claims may be brought under health and safety, anti-discrimination, duty of care and the full range of legislation bearing on the school as workplace, as well as on its having a duty of care to the children in the school. Of course, all this legislation applied prior to 'academisation' and the founding of company schools. The big difference is that, then, complaints were usually dealt with by local authority lawyers, working in conjunction with church bodies in the case of voluntary aided schools. Now, company schools are spending increasing amounts on legal fees.

Legal fees and other expenses are recorded in the annual financial accounts which company schools (academies) and multi-academy trusts (companies combining several schools) are required to file at Companies House. These are free to view online. Annual legal charges often run to tens of thousands of pounds, particularly in the case of multi-academy trusts.

Towards the end of these sets of financial accounts, there is usually an item headed 'related party disclosures'. The purpose of such 'disclosures' is to point up transactions between the company school and trading companies in which those who govern the company school have an interest, especially a financial interest. For example, a company school may lease premises from a company whose directors include members and/or directors of a multi-academy trust. So, by way of an actual example, we see in the full accounts to 31 August 2015 of the Djanogly Learning Trust, based in Nottingham, under note 27, 'Related party transactions':

'... The Trust has entered into leases to enable the Trust to use certain property and other assets owned by the Nottingham City Technology College Trust at a nominal rent. The Trustees of Djanogly Learning Trust are also trustees of the Nottingham City Technology College Trust. At 31 August 2015 Djanogly Learning Trust owed the Nottingham City Technology Trust £32,500 (2014(£6,809)). Nottingham City Technology College Trust has purchased a building at the year-end which has been leased to Djanogly Learning Trust for educational purposes ...'

Hereby hangs a tale. The first company schools were the city technology colleges, opened with private sponsorship and outside of local authority control in the 1980s, under Mrs Thatcher and Kenneth Baker as education secretary of state. These were the models for New Labour's relatively limited academy programme, which has ballooned into current Conservative government proposals to abolish local authority schools altogether and the remaining voluntary aided ones, replacing them with company schools, usually as part of so-called 'multi-academy trusts', bringing together several schools in one legal entity.

Company school accounts also record the number of employees whose emoluments fell within certain bands. Thus, the Djanogly Learning Trust 2015 accounts record that one employee was paid between £120,001 and £130,000. Around this time, another Nottinghamshire-based multi-academy trust paid remuneration of between £270,000 and £275,000 to one employee, and between £115,000 and £120,000 to two others. Who determines these salaries? What external scrutiny is there?

Since 2012, the Education Funding Agency has published 13 reports of investigations into concerns about the use of academy funding. The reports detail a range of inadequate procedures and inappropriate uses of public money, as well as apparently fraudulent behaviour on the part of some persons in influential positions within academies. Are these investigations the tip of an iceberg? Company schools are now big business, which is set to grow much larger. Rather than 'critical friends', school governors now assume the legal responsibilities of company directors and charity trustees.

Many of our schools have already become businesses in the legal sense. Under present proposals, very many more are destined to do so. This inevitably impacts on pay, conditions and terms of employment in schools for all who work there. Is this conducive to the good education of our children? Does it encourage the vocation to teach?

www.gov.uk/government/organisations/companies-house
www.gov.uk/government/collections/academies-investigation-reports

13

Together we are strong
The story of a community campaign
Jill Huish & Gawain Little

This chapter explores an ongoing local community campaign against the closure of all 44 children's centres in Oxfordshire. The National Union of Teachers has been involved as a key partner in the campaign since September 2015, and we wanted to explore both the successes of the campaign and the nature of the relationship between the union and the community campaign. What follows is our account of the campaign so far. As it is ongoing, we cannot yet draw any definitive conclusions about successes and failures but, hopefully, it provides the opportunity to explore how union-community campaigns can run in practice. Most of the chapter is jointly written, but we felt it was important initially to hear each of our voices individually. We have made it clear which one of us is speaking in this first section.

Different starting points

Jill: At the end of June 2015, I heard my local children's centres were once again facing the threat of closure. I'd had a little press involvement and joined protests back in 2013 when Oxfordshire's children's centres had been earmarked for closures before. Back then, I was still recovering from almost a decade with the violent father of my baby. My local children's centres had worked hard to help me escape and their support and the domestic abuse services they offered had saved my life. The thought of myself and of others in similar situations losing our support scared me and angered me in equal measure.

As soon as I heard that Oxfordshire County Council was planning closures again, I contacted the organisers of the small but successful campaign from two years previous. They told me straightaway that they were unable to participate or lead a campaign due to family commitments. Then a local councillor told me not to wait to join a campaign, but start one. So, with the help of a fellow children's centre user in Banbury, I started to create and distribute simple leaflets encouraging people to join the Facebook page and group I'd set up.

These simple things were a struggle without my own computer or printer but I did a lot on my smart phone and called in favours all over. Over the summer I bothered people at children's play days, festivals, town fairs, and anywhere I could get away with pushing leaflets. The local press were keen straightaway and I did a few newspaper articles as well as local television and radio. I attended a county council children's centres stakeholder meeting in August 2015 in my capacity as Advisory Group chair for my local Banbury centres. The Council were vague, but their intention to remove some, if not all, universal services was becoming very clear. Finally, my leafleting and emailing everyone and anyone started to pay off and people started to offer their help and experience through the Facebook group.

Local mums and dads from in and around Oxford joined the campaign first and set up daytime meetings near local children's centres. Local Labour councillors started to offer support and one arranged a meeting space at Oxford Town Hall for what was to be a crucial evening meeting at the end of August 2015. The meeting was well attended and filled with centre users and governors, childcare professionals, doctors, health visitors, union representatives and local councillors. I handed out a few homemade campaign badges with our logo and we invited people to the protests we were organising for the upcoming Oxfordshire County Council meetings at County Hall. We got our first campaign donations as a hat went round and our campaign email list grew considerably. By the end of August we had a simple webpage and links to download and print posters and leaflets.

Gawain: The National Union of Teachers has been in a period of significant change for the past twelve years, which has intensified since the election of the Tory-led Coalition Government in 2010 and its Tory successor in 2015. Faced with an extreme government, determined to achieve the full fragmentation of the education system and the imposition of a market approach based on choice and competition, along with significant attacks on pay and pensions driven by the same agenda, the union has embarked on a significant programme of renewal. This programme is based on three key areas: a grassroots organising strategy, an increased emphasis on community coalition building, and the articulation of an alternative vision for education.

In 2014, following three years of pensions campaigning, alongside other teacher and public sector unions and, from 2013 onwards, a rolling programme of joint action with National Association of Schoolmasters Union of Women Teachers (NASUWT), the NUT found itself in an isolated position. Its key partner, the NASUWT, pulled out of a programme of joint strike action over pensions, pay and workload, with the NUT announcing alone a day of strike action. The NUT response was to reorient its focus towards parents and the wider community with the launch of the *Stand Up for Education* campaign.

Whilst this might look like a sudden decision, it was in fact the culmination of months of discussion on the union's National Executive and amongst grassroots activists. It built on an orientation towards parents and the wider community which has been present, though not so explicit, in the NUT's work for decades, and on discussions that were taking place internally about the future of the union.

The Oxfordshire Association began to implement in earnest this agenda in 2012, with the launch of a local organising plan and a number of new initiatives to develop stronger workplace organisation and greater membership involvement. Local campaigning and political intervention has focused on alternatives to the government's limited vision for education and the Association, like many over the country, spent the first four months of 2015 organising around the NUT's *Stand Up for Education* election manifesto.

In terms of community coalition building, the union was deeply involved in a local anti-academy campaign in 2010/11 which saved a primary school from closure, and has participated in broad local alliances such as the Oxfordshire Anti-Cuts Alliance and the Oxford People's Assembly. However, there has been an increasing recognition that a deeper and more sustainable alliance with parents on issues of education is necessary; that we need to make community unionism a part of our everyday practice.

When I received an email from a local Labour councillor in late August 2015, inviting us to participate in an evening meeting about children's centre closures, this seemed an ideal opportunity both to do some good for local children and families, and to put the principles of our approach into practice.

Jill: Our first protest at the full meeting of Oxfordshire County Council in early September 2015 was well attended. I spoke candidly to the council about the madness of their plans to close all the centres in order to replace them with a handful of referral-only hubs. I raised the dangers families could face without vital preventive services.

The next day the campaign team and a few new members met in a quiet pub in Oxford. We made decisions about creating a clearer campaign logo, starting a bank account to receive funds we'd been offered from local unions and other groups, taking on specific campaign roles, and setting up sub groups to get certain tasks done. Attending his first campaign meeting, Gawain offered support from the NUT and advice on campaigning.

Gawain: Unfortunately, I was not able to attend the evening meeting due to a clash with a union meeting in London. The NUT's local President did attend, and the first campaign meeting I attended was a few days later, in a local pub at lunchtime.

I was deeply impressed when I entered the room to find 20-30 mums of under 5s (there was one other dad in the room), one local activist and filmmaker, and one Labour councillor, deep in a strategic conversation about how to apply pressure to the local council. I said little at the meeting, except to promise a donation from the local union and volunteer to help write a press release and wording for a petition, but I left with a strong sense of the diversity, commitment and vibrancy of the campaign.

Breadth and balance

Among the decisions taken at this meeting were agreements to call a protest at the County Council Cabinet meeting the following week and to set up a petition about saving the centres. Both of these decisions were to have a significant effect on the campaign and how it developed.

That Friday, a small working group of volunteers met to produce a draft text for the petition and plan the protest. Whilst most of us expected to spend the bulk of the time on logistics for the protest, 80 per cent of the meeting was actually spent drafting the petition text. As soon as we began to kick around bits of wording, we realised that we were, in effect, agreeing the fundamental basis of the campaign. We had to work out what the key features of children's centres were and why it was important to save them. Was it the geographical spread of services? Was the open access? Was it the use of professional staff? Was it the co-ordination of the centres at a countywide level? Or their ability to adapt to serve diverse local communities? Clearly, no centre was alike and yet they are all part of a co-ordinated service. Or was it the nature of key services such as breastfeeding support or the Freedom Programme, which works with women who have been victims of domestic violence?

Of course, it was all of this and more but we soon realised that we needed to develop some agreed bottom lines and to make them as general and universally applicable as possible. The more specific we were about the importance of particular services or particular centres, the more chance there was of our message appealing only to a small group who used those services or those centres. At the same time, we needed a level of specificity as we were aware that service users were much more likely to be willing to fight for a service or centre that they valued than a general ideal, however morally right. For us, this was a question of scale. We needed to be able to operate at two different levels at the same time.

The process of decision-making was interesting because, whilst writing by committee is supposed to be a nightmare, we found the experience to be positive. The process was lengthy but it was a positive, collaborative dialogue in which all group members participated, developing, clarifying and occasionally disputing each other's statements. One working group member kept a regularly revised 'current version' on a laptop throughout the discussion and read it to us periodically. When we finished, we had a statement which was based on a demand to retain all 44 centres, with universal provision at each centre, provided by professional staff not volunteers. This became the underlying demand of the campaign, around which we unified service users, staff, unions and supporters.

Someone suggested we put the petition online with 38 Degrees and paper copies were printed. 24 hours after we launched the petition, it had 4,000 signatures and we were ready to take our message out further.

We had also agreed to march through Oxford to County Hall and protest outside the Council's cabinet meeting the following week and that as many of us as possible would put in a request to speak at the meeting. We agreed we wanted the protest to be as diverse as possible and to really represent the breadth of people using children's centres. We put out publicity for a 'family-friendly' march, specifically encouraging those with toddlers and breastfeeding mothers to participate.

Over 150 people marched with us through Oxford, many entering the public gallery for the Council's cabinet meeting. 13 people shared personal stories in powerful speeches in support of Oxfordshire's Children's Centres. In many ways, these were the counterweight to the general nature of the petition. By founding our campaign on a general basis in defence of all centres and all services, but gathering and promoting people's individual testimonies of the difference particular centres or services had made to them, we were able to operate at both a general and a specific scale, at an Oxfordshire level and the level of each local centre. The local press were fully on board by now, covering the protest on the local news and printing articles several times a week.

Getting creative

Somewhat predictably, the Tory cabinet voted in support of plans to close the centres and started to set out a rough timetable for a public consultation ahead of budgetary decisions in the New Year. We started sharing links to help people write to their local councillors and MPs, warning the Council would seek to divide us, and encouraging Oxfordshire to fight for all services together. However, we had several debates of our own to resolve. The first was whether or not to engage with the consultation. It had been the position of the campaign since the proposals had first been drafted that we would not engage with any consultation on the basis that it started from a premise with which we could not agree: cuts to the Early Intervention Service which comprised the children's centres and Early Intervention Hubs. Indeed, from the start of the process, the consultation seemed to be a rigged game. There was no question over whether there would be drastic cuts to the service (£8m, £6m of which had already been agreed in budgetary decisions) and, when the consultation was first launched, there wasn't even a space to suggest alternatives to the council's three options for making the cuts, just a tick-box question asking which you supported (this was later rectified by the addition of an 'other' box).

Nevertheless, a number of campaign members were starting to get concerned that if we didn't engage, the Council might dismiss our protests as a small minority, using a low consultation response as evidence that our views were not shared by most service users. This was a difficult one. Would participating legitimise a consultation that was clearly rigged from the beginning, or would failure to participate undermine our arguments? As before, it was the decision-making process that was crucial here. The campaign had continued to hold regular campaign meetings at which anyone with an interest in saving the centres was welcome. These were the authoritative voice of the campaign and made all the key strategic decisions. The petition and protest working group had evolved into a more general body – just 'the working group' – but decision-making power still rested with the wider campaign meetings.

After thorough debate in a series of full campaign meetings, the decision was made to participate both through a formal campaign response and by encouraging as many individual responses to the consultation as possible. Given the nature of the consultation – a long document which repeatedly put the Council's preferred options and asked leading questions designed to elicit a specific response – we knew we needed a way of making participation easy and of sharing the campaign's alternative viewpoint. It was out of this that the idea of 'consultation packs' or 'action packs' later developed.

Another debate was whether or not we should call a larger protest march on a Saturday. Whilst some in the group felt this was necessary to reach those, particularly teachers and children's centre workers, who were not able to attend protests at council meetings during the day, others felt that it might be a distraction or misdirection of energies. Some feared that many of our core supporters, who had never been involved in political or community campaigning before, might be alienated by what was perceived as a 'militant' tactic. This was not helped by the bureaucratic process of obtaining permissions for public protests from the police, local council and local businesses.

Again, a collective position was reached through discussion at full campaign meetings and, whilst it was agreed that we would go ahead with a march, we emphasised in the publicity the family-friendly nature of the event and arranged the timings around typical feeding times for toddlers and breastfeeding babies. The event we planned was far broader in terms of appealing to our target groups, specifically because of the input of those who were initially unsure about marching. In part, we feel that was possible because of the approach taken to decision-making by all involved in the campaign. As a group, we emphasised group cohesiveness and building the internal strengths of the campaign as much as external outcomes. Personally, we were both in support of marching but remember discussing with each other before a crucial meeting that the most important outcome was that a collective decision be made that everyone felt comfortable with, even if it meant not going ahead with a march.

Everything comes at once

Moving into November 2015, things became very busy very quickly. The march was fast approaching and we needed to use it, and the publicity the campaign had already generated, to maximise the number of responses to the consultation. We decided the only way to do this was to make the consultation as easy as possible to reply to, to give service users a chance to make their voices heard. So we produced our 'consultation packs' which quickly became known as 'action packs'. These were packs which contained a copy of the consultation reply form and a freepost envelope, along with a campaign flyer, 2-side information sheet, poster and two petition sheets, and a step-by-step guide to completing the consultation. We managed to get 500 of these printed and delivered the day before the march, using a printing contact from the NUT.

At the same time, consultation meetings were beginning across the county. We ensured that there were campaign members at each of these, challenging, taking detailed notes and, of course, distributing 'action packs'. Over the course of these meetings, we saw the Council's arguments shift from trying to justify the effectiveness of the proposed replacement for children's centres to admitting, in the words of the Director of Children's Services, that:

'What we have got as a County Council is a set of responsibilities and duties that we can't meet ... Will it impact in the medium term on what will happen to this Council in terms of the consequences, very probably yes, no doubt about that. But the alternative isn't there.'

At the beginning of November, we also had our first opportunity to test the political impact of our campaign. The leader of the Greens on the County Council, seconded by a Liberal Democrat councillor, put a motion to full Council on 3rd November, calling on the Cabinet to 'remove from any future budget options that might involve the closure of any of the children's centres'. The Labour group on the council seemed divided on the issue. Whilst some had given wholehearted support to the campaign, others argued that, as a £6m cut had already been included in budgetary decisions (which they had opposed), there was little that could now be done except to oppose the additional £2m. This added lobbying of opposition councillors to our campaign to-do list, but the extra effort proved worth while.

On 3rd November 2015, the motion was lost 32-30 with one abstention, with all opposition councillors (Labour, Liberal Democrat, Green, and one Independent) voting in favour. It was now clear that, in order to win a reprieve for the centres, we needed to break the majority of the ruling Conservative-Independent Alliance (which included the other three independents on the council).

A few days before the march, something significant came to light.

The Member of Parliament for Witney, Prime Minister David Cameron, echoed his support from 2013 with a statement to BBC Oxford in support of Oxfordshire's children's centres. Mr Cameron clearly stated that he thought the centres should remain open. We made use of this in press releases and on social media at the time but thought little else of it. We then became aware of the existence of correspondence between the Conservative leader of the council and the Prime Minister regarding the cuts. As a campaign, we were obviously keen to know what was in such correspondence. A few days before our march, the campaign received copies of two letters, one from the Prime Minister regarding Oxfordshire's budget briefing and one from the Leader of the Council in response. In these letters, they disputed each other's figures. The Prime Minister lobbied strongly for the retention of children's centres in his local area, saying he was 'disappointed' by the long list of cuts, and the Leader of the Council pointed out that, having campaigned for a Conservative majority and being 'fully supportive' of reducing public expenditure in Oxfordshire, the only way to deliver this national austerity programme and a balanced budget was to cut the children's centres.

The story was quickly picked up by the national media and at Prime Minister's Questions. We followed up with an open letter inviting Mr Cameron to join our march, which was widely shared on social media and printed in full in the *Morning Star.*

The march itself was a huge success, drawing together a wide range of supporters on a wet and windy November day, including groups who had travelled from across the county to be there. All 500 'consultation packs' were given out on the day and lots of people requested additional copies for schools, children's centres, community groups, Labour Party branches and more.

In the weeks following the march, we printed and distributed another 500 consultation packs, local marches and protests sprung up in a number of other locations in response to our central march and, as we got into December, we began to hear rumours that the Council had received record numbers of consultation responses, some even suggesting it might be as high as a thousand. Behind the scenes, the Unite branch representing workers in the centres and

Early Intervention Hubs had met and agreed to ballot for strike action in the New Year.

We now set our minds to how we would identify and persuade individual politicians to support our campaign.

Building unity and getting political

As the New Year began, we had a large number of consultation responses (possibly more than a thousand) and a clear idea of the political division on the Council, but the consultation was closing on 10 January 2016, with a full budget meeting on 16 February, and a decision on children's centres on 23 February. We urgently needed to convert all the hard work we had done into actual progress in shifting councillors.

This was complicated by the fact that the Council had been running a simultaneous consultation on another 98 cuts it proposed to make to everything from school support to adult social care and rural bus subsidies. Oxfordshire County Council had scheduled three 'Talking Oxfordshire' events in late October and early November, evening meetings held around the county for the public to give feedback and question the council. We promoted these meetings heavily on Facebook and produced posters encouraging children's centre users to attend and make their opposition to closures clear. When the Council announced they were to be ticketed events we quickly spread the word and shared information on how people could get tickets. However, up to this point, we had not developed a close working relationship with any of the other campaigns that had emerged.

During the course of our own campaign, we developed a kind of motto that appeared on most of our posters and publicity: 'Together we are strong!' We realised that this was a perfect opportunity to put it into practice, not just for those fighting children's centre closures but also for those fighting all local cuts. With the help of a local Labour councillor, we put together an evening meeting in Oxford Town Hall with speakers from a number of different anti-cuts campaigns including homelessness and housing support, bus users, adult social care campaigners, and the local trades council and People's Assembly group.

After some initial contributions from each campaign, the meeting broke into workshops to discuss what the links were between different campaigns and how we could take forward joint work. The discussion showed not only the level of support for each other's campaigns but also how intricately linked they were. For example, the closure of rural children's centres was made infinitely more dangerous by cutting rural bus subsidies, isolating young families.

It was in our tactics and responses that there was more diversity. A wide range of tactics was shared and debated and a useful discussion was had about the balance between putting pressure on the local council and targeting national government, although general agreement was reached that we should do both. A list was built up of those from different campaigns who wanted to try and co-ordinate activity to enhance the strength of each individual campaign. This is likely to be a future source of strength as the campaign goes forward.

At around this time, we received the results of the consultation. More than 2,700 people had responded, surpassing even our own expectations, with the vast majority in total opposition to the County Council's proposals. We knew the support was out there. We had to mobilise it one more time before the vote. That's where the pledge campaign came in.

The pledge campaign was our answer to two different questions. The first was simple: how do you maximise pressure on elected councillors when their party is the one making the cuts? What is stronger than party loyalty?

The second question was more complex. It was to do with the timescales of the campaign and our chances of winning. The timing was all wrong for us. As Council leader Ian Hudspeth said in his letter to David Cameron,

'I am, of course, also conscious of the 2017 council elections which, in my mind, suggests we should be seeking to take the tricky decisions as soon as we can.'

The further we were from the 2017 local elections, the less vulnerable the councillors taking the decisions were. In addition, we were up against it time wise with budget day looming and a tight timescale for a final decision on the centres. We were worried that, after these key votes, the campaign would lose momentum as people would feel we had already lost. Gawain remembered a conversation with retired Industrial Relations Professor, Mike Ironside, in which Mike argued that political education was the deciding factor in how people responded to losing a battle. Without political education, people tend to become disheartened and either blame themselves or the process of campaigning itself for the loss. Either way, they give up. Once people develop an understanding of how power works in society, rather than be disheartened by a loss, they see it in the context of a massive power imbalance and even more reason to keep fighting to shift the balance of power. They pick themselves up, dust themselves off, and enter the fray again, a little wiser and potentially a little stronger.

So we needed a tactic that would both politicise the campaign and close the gap between February 2016 and May 2017. We decided to start a pledge campaign. We would ask people to sign a pledge that they would not vote, in 2017, for any councillor who voted for the closure of Oxfordshire's children's centres.

The pledge came as a three-part form with a pledge card to keep, a signed section for the campaign to post to your local councillor on your behalf, and a details section to allow the campaign to contact you and let you know how your councillor voted. Anyone could sign the pledge, but we came up with a plan to target the five most vulnerable Conservative councillors in a seat where Labour or the Liberal Democrats were in second place. The two of us set out on a road trip (with children) on Gawain's day off to film parents outside children's centres taking the pledge on Gawain's mobile phone. A campaign supporter who also runs a professional video editing business then put together a short promo video using footage of parents from Witney and Chipping Norton children's centres which we shared on social media to launch the pledge campaign.

Over the next two weeks, we had the pledge running online and regular weekend and weekday stalls in our five target areas: Witney, Chipping Norton, Bicester, Abingdon and Didcot. In just two weeks, we collected over 2,500 pledges from people who were willing to use their vote to protect their local children's centre. These were sent to councillors the weekend before the budget vote with a covering letter announcing our intention to continue collecting pledges over the next 15 months and to communicate regularly with those making the pledge over how to use their vote in 2017. Meanwhile, Unite received its ballot result and announced strike action for 16 February 2016, the day of the budget vote.

A week before the vote, we announced what was to become another national media story. One of the signatures on our petition was that of David Cameron's mother. She had been asked to sign by her sister, who had been attending our protests since near the beginning of the campaign and had been at the joint anti-cuts meeting in Oxford Town Hall. This time, we decided to release the story to the *Mirror*, the *Oxford Mail* and the *Morning Star* at the same time to ensure the story went national whilst retaining the relationship with the papers that had given us such positive coverage throughout. Once again, the story received wide publicity, gaining us a second round of national frontpage stories. All was looking well for the meeting on 16 February.

Then, a few days before the budget vote, when the majority of pledges had been sent, we were thrown another curveball. Whilst the Green Party had put down a budget amendment which removed any options involving the closure of children's centres, the Labour Party had put down an amendment which simply opposed the additional £2m cut but left the original £6m cut in place. Unlike November 2015, when we had the opposition parties united in defence of the centres but not enough pressure on the ruling alliance, we now had plenty of pressure on the Tories but no agreement between opposition parties.

Again, our short-notice decision-making apparatus went into full swing and the usual two or three campaign emails a day went up at least tenfold, along with phone calls and other messages. Some favoured taking a strong line with Labour and explicitly backing the Green amendment on the eve of the budget, others argued we should throw our weight behind Labour as theirs was the only pragmatic approach. Tensions ran high, particularly as personal party affiliations became part of the argument but, in the end, we reached agreement around an approach that maintained pressure for a complete rejection of the cuts but left us with tactical flexibility after the vote not to be campaigning against all but the two Green councillors come 2017, which would have significantly weakened the threat posed by our pledge.

On the evening before the decision, the media started reporting that one of the independent councillors had broken with the alliance. The following morning, as we were gathered outside County Hall with striking Unite workers and campaigners from all of the groups opposing cuts, a second independent councillor announced that he might be having second thoughts about the vote. This constituted the two votes we needed to overturn the Conservative-Independent Alliance majority. Part way through the budget meeting, the Leader asked for an adjournment to discuss the budget with the leaders of other political groups, the first adjournment of a Council meeting since 1997.

The final budget that emerged included the Labour amendments, which reduced the children's centre cuts by £2m, cuts to adult social care by £2m, and a number of other measures. Whilst this was not an unqualified success for the campaign, it was a significant victory. The fight ahead of us is likely to be over how the £2m is spent, ensuring it goes towards meeting our initial demands.

What next?

The narrative above describes our experience of a campaign which we feel has been strong and cohesive and, whilst still far short of our eventual aim, has won real gains for children and families in Oxfordshire.

The success of the campaign so far has rested in particular on our decision-making structure. All key decisions are taken at regular, open meetings to which everyone interested in saving the centres is welcome. When decisions have to be taken by a smaller group because of speed or confidentiality, they feel a strong sense of accountability to the wider group, knowing that all decisions will be reported back and discussed and that the wider group has the final say.

The breadth of people involved in the campaign has given the group both a wide tactical repertoire and a good knowledge of the landscape it is operating in. The combination of staff and governors from children's centres, trades unionists, academics and educationists, councillors, campaigners, and children's centre users is at times quite overwhelming in the depth and breadth of its knowledge. And, of course, the final categories include people from all walks of life. What they have in common is very young children.

This was another facet to the campaign: most of us were campaigning around full or part time parenting duties. We both have two children age five and under, who would regularly accompany us to meetings and protests, and this was quite common within the campaign. People would also drop in or out of activity as they went on maternity or paternity leave, had children, and went back to work. However, this in itself helped to create an environment where it was fine to have limited availability because of children's eating or sleeping routines, where it was fine to commit for a period of time before life intruded.

Motivation and common cause runs throughout our campaign. From those for whom the centres are livelihood and a service they have developed over many years, to those for whom it is a lifeline, the strength of commitment to the centres is total. This has been a massive strength as, whenever problems or pitfalls have arisen, the commitment exists to overcome these rather than to give up or fragment the group.

The campaign came across the problem of scale early on in the need to be both general and Oxfordshire-wide and to be specific and local. At several points, these seemed to conflict, most notably when we came across groups founded to save a particular centre or service. However, it was obvious that this was the main way in which people would engage with the campaign and, if we were able to establish working relationships with these groups, they would fulfil the role of 'local broker groups', trusted partners in the local area that allow the campaign to engage people at an individual level whilst remaining general and universal in its appeal.

In part, this came from the NUT's prior experience of involvement in the Save Oxfordshire Libraries Campaign. At the time, Gawain was President of the Trades Council and Chair of the Oxfordshire Anti-Cuts Alliance, which had managed to bring together almost 40 different local library groups in co-ordination against a similar cut. The tension had been ever-present in that campaign, too. Part of the solution was having effective deliberative structures that gave partner organisations a voice.

Throughout the campaign, we try to invest in organisational structures and relationships, at times prioritising the health of the campaign over external objectives. Developing strong working relationships and a cohesive yet robustly deliberative campaign has been a conscious effort. Within this, we have worked hard to balance the role of the union with the role of other partners, particularly at key points such as when resources were needed to produce materials such as banners and placards for demonstrations, or consultation packs, as we felt there was a danger that the voice holding the chequebook might dominate. Throughout the campaign, union representatives have engaged in full campaign meetings with the same voice as anyone else, and financial donations have been made through a separate process.

The involvement of the union brings a lot to the campaign. It does so in terms of resource, including financial support and some involvement from a paid organiser, but also in terms of broadening the tactical repertoire of the group and providing links to other supportive constituencies. It would be a very different campaign without the involvement of Oxfordshire NUT.

At the same time, the collaboration has been incredibly valuable for the union, particularly in developing stronger links with the local parent community, but also the way in which it has changed the union activists who are involved. As Amanda Tattersall argues in the context of Australia,

'coalitions are a source of power for unions, not simply because they supplement a union's objectives with the resources of another organisation but because they can help renew unions. This kind of strength requires a sometimes challenging kind of reciprocal coalition building. Yet this slower, stronger coalition practice can help unions rebuild their internal capacity, develop new leaders, and innovate how they campaign. Coalitions can also shift unions from being agents focused on the workplace to becoming organisations that connect workplace concerns with a broad agenda that in turn can transform the broader political climate.'

As Allan Flanders (1970) expressed it,

> 'coalitions allow unions to act not only in their "vested interests" but with a "sword of justice".'

We fight on to save Oxfordshire's children's centres and, as we do so, we strengthen our organisations and their capacity to stand up for children and families in Oxfordshire.

Together we are strong!

www.saveoxfordshireschildrenscentres.com

14

Enough is enough

Julie James

'I like coming to school because when you're at home you feel bored. I'm glad that we come to school because when I grow up I want to be a teacher. The subjects I like best at school are English …' (Me, aged 9, January 25th 1972)

I remember it vividly. Nine years old, sitting in a classroom full of sunshine and the tingly smell of powder paint listening to the teacher read to us from a Leon Garfield novel. I think it might have been *Smith.* I was so engrossed in the story it took me a few seconds to register what happened … My teacher just swore in front of the whole class! She read the word, 'bloody' in front of a class of 9 and 10 year olds! My initial reaction was one of shock, disbelief. I must have misheard? Stifled giggles around the room told me I did hear it correctly. I was stunned.

But at that moment an idea lit up in my head that was to be my beacon for the next 43 years. It struck me there and then that *I* could become a teacher. *I* could read to children, captivate them and then make them jump or giggle or think or dream … For a girl from a council estate with a dad who was a labourer and a mum who worked in a garage, the idea seemed ridiculous. But, and here is where my story really begins, teachers believed in me, nurtured me, inspired me and that is why I now have to stand up for education.

'Airoplanes are schececduled/ For loads of flights/ But on a different note/ I love your tights.' (a pupil's poem, spellings from the original)

I *loved* so many of my teachers because they were creative and funny. Yes, they taught me so well that I achieved excellent results. But I never felt that this was the only important thing. In my thirty one year long career I have witnessed a huge increase in over-testing and seen the pressure of school league tables taking precedence over the needs of individual pupils. In my current job I work with pupils who are quite clearly the victims of this narrow focus, pupils who are anxious, present challenging behaviour, who are phobic or who have an Autistic Spectrum Disorder (ASD), many of whom have been excluded or are at risk of exclusion because they are perceived as a threat to the school's results and too expensive to support effectively within mainstream.

'Dearest Miss James. I am away because I have tonsil lightness.'

Because my teachers believed in me, I never wanted to let them down. I would never have time off even when I was ill. Even now, I haven't had a day off for 13 years because I do not want to let my pupils down. But the stress and pressure of the job now means that I could not and would not ever survive in a mainstream school. I watch as friends who are teachers in mainstream succumb to stress-related illness and even depression, when the stress has overcome them and they crumble.

One of the reasons for the most recent National Union of Teachers' strike was the threat of larger class sizes due to underfunding. The arguments for smaller class sizes are self-evident and the small class sizes of expensive private schools attest to this. Even with only twenty five pupils in a class, five lessons a day in secondary school, that's one hundred and twenty five pupils to give individual attention to, to plan for, to mark books meaningfully for. And that's before all the recording and assessment and target setting. Just writing it down now, it seems absurd that anyone would think that this is manageable. Now add 10 more pupils to the class ....

'Also, the reason that you're so good is not just that you're funny and caring, it actually feels like we mean something, that we're not just grades on a table, that we're actually equal.' (written in a thank-you letter from a pupil)

No government minister or Office for Standards in Education (Ofsted) expert is ever going to persuade me that 'caring' is not a vital part of being a good teacher. But caring is not quantifiable, it cannot be measured and inputted on a spreadsheet and displayed in an impressive-looking paper exercise for Ofsted to scrutinize. For many of the pupils I teach, a teacher or teaching assistant might be one of the first adults who has shown them respect, care and belief. When I used to work in a Secure Unit, teenagers would arrive from the most traumatic and damaging lives and, within months, sometimes weeks, the love and dedication of the care teams and education team would begin to soften their hard exteriors and they would begin to thrive.

'Students who are loved at home, come to school to learn, and students who aren't, come to school to be loved.' (Ferroni)

I have to stand up for education because it is not just the A* to C grade pupils that matter; it is the other pupils, the vast majority of pupils who may never achieve a C but who might achieve two G grades and be thrilled, because they didn't learn to read until they were 14; or who might not achieve any GCSE grades but who might secure a place at college to do hairdressing or mechanics and be delighted, because their mental health problems were so severe that they had been hospitalized. And it is not just the academic pupils that matter. We know that we all have different teaching and learning styles and that many pupils with learning difficulties such as dyslexia or pupils on the autistic spectrum, can excel or thrive in Arts subjects. But the government cuts to funding mean that many school subjects, particularly in the arts, are being removed from the curriculum. It seems to me immoral to deny less academic pupils opportunities to succeed and instead to label them as failures because they do not attain the 'magical' A* to C grades.

'You look so cute when you're asleep. I'm sorry that you're sick and I wish you weren't. I went to see Jurassic Park on Saturday. It's so quiet today it's like being in a graveyard except for a few nutters …' (letter from a pupil, written in class)

I was probably around 27, teaching a Year 8 class and gradually, my headachey, sicknessy feeling began to take over. The class were engrossed in their writing and not needing me much so I said, 'I am just going to rest my head on the desk for a few moments. Let me know if you need me.' The next thing I knew, it was the end of the lesson. A girl had gently woken me up to tell me. They had all packed away and were tiptoeing out, leaving me a giant card made of display paper with a drawing of me asleep and my head of department shouting 'You're fired!! You're fired!!' They had written me lovely 'get well' messages and funny drawings.

Thinking back on that story now, I see that because they trusted me, I could trust them. They knew I would always do right by them, always care and do my best. And in return they showed me care and respect and behaved themselves.

Successive governments have not trusted teachers and this one trusts them least of all. We must be criticized, undermined, judged, constantly worried, and never, *never* trusted to do what we believe is best for our pupils.

This atmosphere of distrust is toxic and dangerous and has led to me needing to step down. But it has also given me more energy to fight for the profession I love. And now that I don't need to project my voice in classrooms anymore it is even stronger and louder to shout for education.

15

The real 'pay' and 'conditions'

Rosie Hancock

My journey into teaching was unexpected, but all being well, I will retire having served, and also contributed to, a diverse and emotionally intelligent society that values the sanctity of children. I hope to rest easy knowing that when the mountain rumbled and the dragon threatened to breathe fire over the world, that I fought alongside many others for what was right. This is not a political threat I talk of, it is a moral one.

As dramatic as the aforementioned statement sounds, I truly believe there is a serious threat to the fundamental experiences of children today. The high-stakes testing regime poses significant risk to the enquiring minds that are moving through our compulsory education system. Too long have teachers been compliant and acquiescent to the unreasonable expectations of the higher powers with their predetermined competencies! Enough is now truly enough!

Clarity is needed around a number issues related to teachers' 'pay and conditions'. This clarity is important because these issues may be used in the near future to influence public opinion on certain educational debates. There are now significant uncertainties around maternity and sick pay, pay scales and an ever-increasing work load. However, the financial reward and other benefits brought to me by the teaching profession are NOT the fuel for my active role in campaigning to save our state education system. I know that I am not the only professional that shares this view. So, I would like to raise the profile of the real 'pay and conditions' that are burdening teachers across our nation.

I would like to consider 'pay' as the daily exchange between my children and I. This 'pay' can be varied, but not contrived or complicated. Their smiling faces, their compassionate and kind demeanours, their hard work, their attention and their willingness to learn and do themselves, their families and me proud is the celebrated 'capital' in my classroom. How do I 'pay' them? Like many others, I aim to provide a safe and trusting place of learning, filled with the magic of the unknown and the continued wonderment of the known. As a classroom family, together we continue to embed a philosophy that learning can be a personal and individual journey that can be shared and rejoiced in respectfully with others: humankind is diverse by nature. I 'pay' them with a sense of equality; no one is better or more worthy of experiences than anyone else and that one's capacity to acquire knowledge and intelligence are not fixed, but can grow and be nurtured. We 'pay' each other by creating an ethos within the spaces we inhabit that nothing is beyond our reach; that refining our critical thinking and problem solving skills will continue to develop us into emotionally literate contributors in a challenging and ever-changing society (and world).

Such payment creates the 'conditions' that we teachers work in; a wonderful landscape where we marvel in the actions, conversations and consequential discoveries of the children we encounter. However, there comes a time (none more so than this year) when such 'pay' and 'conditions' are compromised because the expectations become prescribed, rigged, unforgiving and elitist. The predetermined levels, set in the context of a narrowed curriculum, become brutish and so out of reach for some children that the seedlings of intellectual wonderment begins to wilt and die.

These are the 'pay and conditions' I fight for. These are the 'pay and conditions' that are under threat from a looming privatised education system that will openly operate using market forces embedding a high-stakes testing regime as its engine house. These are the 'pay and conditions' I will fight for until they are protected.

Children are pawns of this high-stakes testing system, particularly in tested year groups (Year 2 and Year 6). There have always been tests, the scores used to populate school league tables and to set standardised academic markers, but there have never been tests and curriculum content as we see it now.

I was present with two groups of children during their Key Stage 2 Standard Assessment Tests this year. The first group were those children, blissfully unaware of the complex questions, who cruised on regardless. They answered questions quickly and inaccurately due to the nature of the language and without understanding of the questions inference. My smiling face around the classroom was a façade; inside I was crying and telling myself I had failed these children; that the 'pay and conditions' that I had promoted and advocated prior to this event really meant nothing. Such feelings were exasperated when observing the second group of children that initially felt good and confident within the given tested area. When the reality hit that there was simply not enough time for them to work through such challenging questions, heads went down on tables, tears flowed. Alternatively they adopted the approach of the first group which was to answer with their immediate thoughts and not the required carefully considered answer.

The policy makers tell us that new systems have been designed to raise standards. If such standards begin to irradiate a child's motivation and engagement whilst negatively impacting their mental health then I'm going to be challenging and standing boldly by what I consider to be morally right. I'm not politically minded. I'm not as articulate as many others. I sometimes cry out of frustration and despair. I sometimes get flustered when trying to explain my thinking. But then I remember what a real teachers 'pay and conditions' are. I feel the warmth of the children's smiles, the excitement of their questions and feel honoured to be a part of their existence.

I am not alone, I am not scared. As the mountain rumbles and the dragon begins to move, I shall stand shoulder to shoulder with parents, teachers, headteachers and anyone else who believes that the high-stakes testing regime and a proposed forced privatised education system could and, in some cases is, violating the sanctity of childhood.

16

Invest in education

Kevin Courtney

On Tuesday 5 July 2016, teachers across England took strike action in defence of national terms and conditions and against cuts to school funding. This strike marked the opening of an ongoing campaign, including industrial action, in order to halt and reverse government underfunding of education. We all know that schools are facing a very difficult funding situation at the moment. The base reason for that is because the Chancellor froze the money he gives to schools per pupil, while he is increasing the money he takes from schools per member of staff. Increased national insurance costs that governing bodies have to bear, increased teacher pension costs that governing bodies have to bear, all amount to about a five per cent charge on a teacher payroll, so that for every 20 teachers a school employs, they have to find a whole extra salary to give back to the Chancellor of the Exchequer and the Treasury.

The week before the strike, I wrote to the then Secretary of State for Education, setting out the National Union of Teachers' (NUT) concerns on funding and offering to suspend our action if the government agreed to fund schools sufficiently to cover the increased staffing costs that have been imposed on them, tell academies to have regard to national terms and conditions, and engage in meaningful talks to end our dispute. In reply, the then Secretary of State – Nicky Morgan – claimed, 'the schools budget has been protected in real terms going forward'.

If that is the case, then why has the Institute for Fiscal Studies estimated that school funding will have fallen by about eight per cent over five years by 2020?

Why are head teachers telling the NUT that they are experiencing budget cuts, in some cases of hundreds of thousands of pounds next year? Why have 70 per cent of school leaders in a recent survey told the NUT that a lack of funding is affecting education standards in their schools? The Department for Education's claims simply do not stand up to scrutiny.

Declining budgets are leading to real problems in our schools. Class sizes are going up. Many NUT members have told us that they will be teaching classes of 35 from September 2016. Subject choices are reducing because art, drama and dance teachers are being made redundant or not replaced when they leave.

Individual attention is going down, learning support assistants are being dismissed. And in many other cases, teachers' terms and conditions are being reduced. All of these changes are happening because former Chancellor George Osborne refused to fund our schools well enough and he did not do anything to keep pace with inflation.

Nicky Morgan's denials did nothing to change the fate of those teachers and children on the sharp end of this government's policies. And of course these funding cuts are not happening in a vacuum. They take place at a point when the education system is being put under increasing strain by assessment and accountability systems that are unfit for purpose, when excessive testing already skews and narrows the curriculum (a process that will be made worse by funding cuts), and when the government is proposing to spend £1.3 billion on the forced conversion of every school to academy status, removing parental and community accountability at the same time.

Funding cuts also take place alongside a huge increase in child poverty, as the impact of the government's wider economic policies of austerity hits working-class communities. It is not just teachers' terms and conditions at stake here but our children's educational experience and future life chances. Many economists are arguing that one of the consequences of the European Union Referendum result will be a sharp spike in inflation. If this is the case, and if we can't persuade the government that it has to allow school budgets to match inflation, then the situation will be even worse than I have described.

So the NUT's action marks the launch of a campaign to convince the government that it has to invest in education, not cut back on it, and that investment is the right thing to do for our country, for our young people and for our education service. Only by putting that funding in can we protect teachers' conditions of service and our children's learning conditions. We are asking support for the NUT's ongoing industrial action as part of a wider campaign to force the government's hand and ensure that teachers' terms and conditions are protected and that our children get the education they deserve.

At the same time, we want to work alongside parents and others to tackle the very real issues within our education system – excessive testing, narrowing of the curriculum, loss of parental involvement in governance. Tackling these issues must go hand in hand with ensuring that the system itself is properly resourced. Let's campaign together for the education investment that can protect teachers' conditions of service and our young people's conditions of learning.

A version of this article appeared in the Morning Star *on 5th July 2016.*

17

The education laboratory

Tom Unterrainer

'Knowledge is the liberator from the empire of natural forces and destructive passions; without knowledge, the world of our hopes cannot be built … The way is clear. Do we love our children enough to take it?'¹ Bertrand Russell, 1926

Writing ninety years ago, Bertrand Russell claimed that 'the way is clear' for those hoping to transform the education system and the educational experiences of young people. Russell argued that knowledge 'wielded' without love or concern for children and young people was an ultimately destructive force in society. He argued for the opposite approach: 'knowledge wielded with love', that could lead to a fundamental transformation of society.

If the way was clear to Russell and his readers, the principles he advocated have yet to be put to the test. For we retain an education system that would in large part be recognisable to Russell. The argument is not about individual teachers and their personal attitudes towards the young people in their care: now, as in the Victorian and post-Victorian age, the vast majority of teachers do their work out of a passion for learning and a deep sense of social responsibility. For example, a survey conducted by the Association of Teachers and Lecturers (ATL) in 2015 found that the top two reasons given for starting a teaching career to be that teachers 'want to make a difference' and 'enjoy working with children and young people'.² The same survey found that the top three responses to the question 'What do you enjoy about teaching?' were: 'working with children', 'light bulb moments' – those times when understanding and inspiration suddenly emerge – and 'helping children enjoy learning'. It is sadly the case that these teachers, whatever the impulses that brought them into teaching and keep them in the profession, labour under circumstances not of their choosing.

In crisis

The education system – the mutating school structures, the constellation of exams and qualifications, methods of teaching and so on – if it has been designed in any meaningful sense, has not been designed with the actual needs of children and young people as a central concern. Love plays no part in the matter. What we have instead is a system that seems to have been established by adaptations to and adjustments by successive phases of political impulse. These range from the 'we must be seen to be doing something' to the 'rip it up and start again' variety. Some of these impulses are well meaning and have had a significant and positive impact – the large-scale investment in buildings and equipment during the 1997-2010 Labour governments, for example. Some are completely destructive.

In general, however, the successive reforms, changes, the fiddling at the edges and repeated tippings out of the baby with the bath water constitute a purely short-term, ill-founded and destructively experimental approach to education. The drivers for this process will be discussed later on, but for now the results will be considered. The education system in this country has reached a real and tangible crisis point. One aspect of this crisis is a complete lack of confidence in the political leadership at the helm of education. This lack of confidence is illustrated by the example of a large groups of head teachers who felt moved to publicly denounce the damage inflicted upon their students.[3]

In May 2016, fifty-seven head teachers from schools in Devon, Plymouth and Torbay penned an open letter to Nicky Morgan – then Secretary of State for Education – and Nick Gibb – Schools Minister – that opened with these words:

> *'We are writing, as a large group of primary school head teachers … to ask that you act now to put a stop to the chaos and resulting damage that your Government is currently inflicting upon children, families and staff involved in education in this country. We call into question the quality of political leadership and lack of coherent vision of the current Government.'*[4]

Another aspect of the crisis is the result of changes to the testing regime for primary school children. In the aftermath of the publication of 2016 Key Stage 2 Standard Assessment Test (SAT) results, teachers and head teachers in Lancaster and Morecambe issued an online petition calling on Nicky Morgan to resign.[5] Part of the petition reads:

'This year 47% of 11-year-old children will be told they haven't reached the "expected" standard in at least one of their SATs papers ... This is extraordinarily demoralising for children ... Nicky Morgan was warned by teachers and head teachers that the criteria for teacher assessment did not allow teachers to recognise the strengths of pupils' work ... A Secretary of State who demands accountability from schools should apply that principle to herself ... Nicky Morgan must first of all apologise to all those children who took KS2 SATs this year, and then resign her post.'[6]

We have yet to see if Morgan's sacking by the new Prime Minister, and her replacement by Justine Greening, results in a necessary change of course. But the lack of confidence in these aspects of the current government's handling of the education system presented itself well before the results of KS2 SAT tests were published. In the run-up to the tests, thousands of parents, carers and their children participated in a widely supported and widely publicised 'Kids' Strike'. Spearheaded by an organisation called 'Let Our Kids Be Kids'[7], the 'strike' was called for 3 May 2016 in support of demands from teachers and head teachers for drastic reforms to the regime of high-stakes testing. More than 8000 people registered online for the 'strike' – and the enrichment activities organised for the striking children by the campaign – and some press reports suggested participation, in one form or another, of up to 40000.[8]

One parent, quoted in *The Daily Telegraph*, explained his reasons for participating in the strike along with his five year old son. Ben Ramalingam said:

'Our kids are being left disengaged and stressed. Kids who previously loved school are now refusing to go. There are a number of people who are saying this has the potential to turn into not just an educational crisis, but a mental health crisis... There is an experiment being run on our children and there is no proof it works. It is really inappropriate and, I think, unethical to do it.'[9]

Parents, teachers and students themselves now know that these KS2 tests are not fair and not fit for purpose. There have been reports from up and down the country of the deleterious impact of the tests on the children who are subjected to them, to the extent that some have suffered real trauma at the hands of this regime. If testing is a symptom of the general crisis in education, it is just one of many symptoms. From funding cuts, increased class sizes, problems with teacher recruitment and retention, lack of confidence in secondary school assessments, reductions in the range of subjects on offer and a growing number of financial and administrative scandals in what were once called 'schools' but are now known by the term 'academies'. We have a system that pays no attention to the real needs of children and young people, a system ignorant of the material and social barriers faced by the majority of learners, a system that has become unmistakably geared towards fulfilling commercial expectations and goals.

If anywhere in the United Kingdom illustrates the profound crisis cooked up in the policy laboratories of Westminster, it is Nottingham.

The Nottingham experiment

On 5 June 2003 the then Minister for Schools, David Miliband MP, visited Nottingham. His purpose was to make a visit to the Djanogly City Technology College (CTC) which was to convert into a City Academy under new provisions outlined in The Education Act 2002. Prior to this Act, CTC's – which were established under provisions in the 1988 Education Reform Act as centrally-funded schools independent of local authority oversite – were not permitted to convert into Academies nor was there provision for the Academy programme to extend into rural areas, to become 'all-age' schools or to open primary or sixth form Academies.

Mr Miliband's trip to Nottingham was indeed an auspicious occasion. Not only because up until this point only three Academies had opened nationwide – in Bexley, Haringey and East Middlesbrough in September 2002 – but because the reasons for his visit opened the door to the effective destruction of locally-controlled, accountable and democratic school organisation in the City of Nottingham.

The story, however, does not start in June 2003. At this point Nottingham already had a mix of 'schools': grant-maintained, CTCs, voluntary aided and community secondary schools. Some of these schools were permitted to set their own admissions policies, some operated what were widely understood to be 'covert' selection processes,[10] some selected components of their intake on the basis of religious observance or aptitude towards certain subjects, whilst what remained admitted all-comers regardless of class, race, religion, perceived ability or postcode. To all intents and purposes, the 'Comprehensive Model' of education had ceased to exist some time before Miliband's visit. The peculiar geography that hemmed the Nottingham Local Authority – the body with overall responsibility for schools and young people's services – into some of the most economically and socially disadvantaged communities in the United Kingdom meant that Nottingham's schools faced significant problems from 1998 onwards when the administration of schools passed from the County Council – which enjoyed the benefits of scale and mix – to the City Council, which had a much more confined pool of experience, resources and resilience.

Economic and social depravation, a 'diversified' school system, and a Local Authority with reduced capacity combined to create the test-bed for New Labour's innovations on the previous Tory government's policy. A key factor in the mix was the existence of a Labour council that now exercised almost complete hegemony over policy making within the bounds of the city. That this same council was widely perceived to be a champion of New Labour policies – the vanguard of Blairism in local government – helped things along somewhat. The Local Authority and a succession of 'Portfolio Holders for Education' – local councillors appointed to oversee schools – husbanded the expansion of academies throughout the city's secondary schools. Local union negotiators, school governors, teachers, parents and communities were assured that there was no alternative to this process if the City was to secure new buildings, increased funding and therefore better life chances for the children and young people of Nottingham. Whilst campaigning against the conversion of a secondary school in Bulwell to an academy, members of the National Union of Teachers were told that 'the school is falling down … have you seen the building? … this is the only way to rebuild the school for our children, of course we support the academy'. Much preparatory work had been done by those seeking to revolutionise Nottingham's schools.

Over a relatively short period of time the number of academies increased, helped along by policies from central government that allowed for the imposition of academy status on schools deemed to be 'failing' by the school inspectorate (Ofsted). This process was undertaken in the name of improving life-chances for the children and young people of the city. One aspect of the mission was to have been the creation of 'specialist' academies catering for specific needs and skill deficiencies in the local jobs market. So Nottingham was to have academies that, along with teaching the core aspects of the National Curriculum, would specialise in 'retail', 'healthcare', 'information technology', 'hospitality' etc… The example of schools and existing academies that had boosted 'attainment' and therefore school league table results by offering more 'vocational' orientated qualifications made this an attractive option for those who take government 'statistics' to be a key measure. At least one 'school' in Nottingham boosted their A*-C GCSE 'pass rates' by offering the equivalent of five GCSEs in information technology. The economic crash of 2007/2008 and the consequent disruptions to the jobs market seem to have halted this particular development, but it did not stop the 'academisation' process. As the number of secondary academies increased, other schools were subjected to increasing pressures to 'academise'. These pressures intensified with the election of the Conservative Party-dominated Coalition Government of 2010-2015 which quite rightly identified the academy programme as a logical extension of previous Tory policies. The new Secretary of State for Education, Michael Gove, extended this policy further by announcing on 26 May 2010 – a mere twenty days after the general election – that all schools would be given the 'freedom' to become academies.[11] Aspects of previous policy were turned on their head. For example, whereas in the past schools judged to be 'failing' would be 'saved' by becoming an academy, now schools judged to be 'outstanding' would have their academy status 'fast-tracked' in order for them to be given the freedoms to become even more 'outstanding' [sic] and to give a helping hand to their 'failing' counterparts.

By the end of October 2013, Nottingham's secondary schools largely conformed to Michael Gove's dream of an academy-dominated system. A majority of the city's secondary schools had 'academised', a number of them had started to group together into what have become multi-academy trusts (MATs) – where 'better performing' academies oversee 'struggling' ones – and the city looked set to open its doors to its first 'Free School', another of Mr Gove's innovations. Then came 12 November 2013. On this date eight teams of inspectors from the Office for Standards in Education (Ofsted) swept into the city to carry out inspections at eight different schools in what the local newspaper termed a 'blitz'.[12] Ofsted inspectors concluded that out of the eight schools inspected, six were 'inadequate' – the lowest possible rating made by Ofsted.

The politics of this situation are difficult to fathom given that half of the schools rated 'inadequate' were already academies and the remaining three were on a course to academisation in the short to medium term. Weren't academies supposed to improve standards? Wasn't policy already in place to encourage all secondary schools to academise? Didn't the 'micro-economy' of Nottingham's school system already have sufficient 'market levers' in place to ensure that complete academisation was only a matter of time? Clearly something was not working out as planned. In an email to Graham Allen, the Member of Parliament for Nottingham North, whose constituency contains one of the 'inadequate' schools, Ofsted explained that they 'wanted to find out why secondary pupils in Nottingham had "consistently underperformed" for several years, compared with those in the rest of the East Midlands and nationally.'[13] If Ofsted and the government had wanted a true, reasonable and measured picture of what was and is happening in Nottingham's schools they might have found a method other than a 'blitz' and the media frenzy surrounding it. It seems clear that they were not interested in such an inquiry. Rather, the mass inspections of Nottingham's schools in November 2013 should be seen as a stunt – part and parcel of Mr Gove's agenda and the agenda of his successors – to demonstrate the efficiency of the academies model.

Within two and a half years something 'miraculous' happened: not only had all but one of the secondary schools in Nottingham converted to an academy – all but two of the city's schools had emerged from 'special measures' as a result of an 'inadequate' Ofsted rating. Within three years of the Ofsted 'blitz' there will be no secondary schools in the city that are not either academies or 'Free Schools' and there will be an ever-increasing number of primary schools converting to academy status. Whilst Ofsted and the government made its point and whilst more Nottingham schools 'escaped the constraints' of local, democratic oversight, the city's teachers, children, young people and communities continued to suffer. The Ofsted blitz and academy bonanza has done nothing to address the endemic poverty in the city, nor have the existing and upcoming cuts to the City Council's budget been cancelled or lessened. No effective measures are in place to address the teacher recruitment crisis in the city, let alone the problems presented by the looming population 'bulge' that is set to impact local schools. Nothing has been done about a curriculum that is increasingly narrow. Ofsted's intervention has not resulted in more sports, arts and humanities lessons. The libraries are not overflowing with books. The school funding crisis has not been solved. Children and young people in this city are no happier, safer or securer as a result. Their job prospects have not been improved as a result of Ofsted's intervention. No love was wielded in Ofsted's blitz. Something is still very wrong in our schools.

Jug and clay, or flower?

'*The young child's mind may be likened to a jug into which the teacher pours information, as much or as little and of the kind that is thought fit … Similarly the child's character is regarded as some plastic material separate from the faculties of the mind, to be moulded into shape … The analogy of the flower suggests an upbringing that enables a person to blossom in his or her own way. The gardener's job is to provide the most appropriate soil and nourishment that he knows of, and to protect the tender plant from extremes of frost and scorching heat.*'[14]

Tony Weaver, 1962

Something interesting and instructive is happening in American schools. To clarify, it's not the hyper-commercialisation, continued segregation, conformity and narrowing of curriculum in that country's state-funded schools that is of interest – although a survey of these processes is essential in understandiing what is happening to schools in England. No, the interesting development in American schooling is the proliferation of fee-paying schools that fundamentally reject the 'jug and clay' view of childhood. Also of interest is the fact that such schools are overwhelmingly popular with sections of the elite in American society. Take the example of an institution named 'Avenues: The World School' based in New York. Megan Erickson describes the school as follows: 'teachers commonly have decades of experience, and turnover is low. Students begin immersion in a second language as pre-schoolers. Student government assemblies convene twice every six days. Discussion is the preferred pedagogy.'[15] This sounds like a progressive dream, does it not? However, there's a catch: 'In the frenzied fever dream of American free-market capitalism, everything is for sale, including education. Tuition at Avenues exceeds $45,000' per year in a city where the median income is $50,711.[16]

Only the rich can afford to send their children to such places, schools where budget cuts, competition, formal assessments, league tables and a narrowing curriculum are unimaginable. These are places where young people blossom in their own ways, where children are cultivated as 'fully developed human beings fit for a variety of labours'.[17] Such places are the preserve of the already privileged. Why so? Why is such an education fit only for a small section of society, people who could choose any school in the world but who prefer – in increasing numbers – a progressive alternative? Why, when they could send their children to the American versions of Eton and Westminster are the CEO's of Google, hedge-fund managers, the directors of big business and those who can only just afford to do so sending their children to such a place? Because when you can buy the best education available on the planet, you buy it. Because when given the opportunity to do the best for their children, parents and carers do the best for them.

Parents, children and educators in the UK are told that high-stakes testing, league tables, invasive inspection and appraisal regimes are the only way to secure the best possible outcomes for young people. We are supposed to believe that a grade C or above in a narrow array of qualifications is the best measure of success. A philosophy of 'train it, measure it, race it' dominates, where children and young people are trapped in a perpetual horse race, where every day is like the Grand National. The children of working class families and others are being sold an educational bill of goods that would horrify not only the elites of New York but ordinary families on much of the European continent. Teachers are told to form and fill jugs. Gardening is not encouraged.

How does this fit into the multiple crises that have already been described? Ken Coates, who documented poverty in Nottingham, argued the following:

> '*It remains true that the liberal educational goals are, at root, in flagrant contradiction to the basic assumptions which regulate our economic life. The result is that today, far from education – individual development in co-operative activity – reaching out through working life to become a life-long experience, it is still true that industry constantly exerts itself to reach its clammy hands down into schools, in order to make wage-slavery as life-long, and as inescapable, as it possibly can.*'[18]

Ken Coates was concerned to identify and celebrate the very many positive and progressive developments in education at the time. For example, the raising of the school leaving age and the 'new spirit in the schools' where '[t]he primary school today … is a place of adventure, experiment, liveliness, joy, and a felicitous co-operation between child, parent and teacher'.[19] But he was also finely tuned into the realities of employment at the time and the contradictions between developments in education and the practicalities of the workplace: '[t]he more co-operative and participatory that teaching techniques become, the more grossly they will be out of phase with the roles for which their victims are being prepared'.[20]

The development of what Tony Simpson describes in this volume as 'Company Schools' – Academies and 'Free Schools' – the high-stakes testing regime that is discussed here and elsewhere, and the general narrowing of the curriculum can be understood as an effort to resolve the contradiction identified by Ken Coates. The mass exodus of teaching professionals, the teacher recruitment crisis, and the avalanche of stress, depression and anxiety amongst children, young people and their teachers are manifestations of this process. In short, there is now little effort made to maintain the pretence that schools are places of liberation, wonderment and joy. The steady progress towards the privatisation of schools and the further regimentations of the curriculum are answers to the oft-posed question: 'what sort of education does modern production require?' In large parts of the world, the 'Global Education Reform Movement' [GERM] is working to provide similar answers to this question. Our children are victims of a global process that only the wealthy elites are able to escape. This is because when we talk of 'modern production' we are talking about the practices of multi-national companies, firms that operate within a global market with global competition and global imperatives. We are talking about zero-hours contracts, anti-union laws, employment practices geared towards avoiding payment of the minimum or living wage. We are talking about short-termism, precariousness and uncertainty. When asked the question 'what sort of education does modern production require?', Michael Gove, Nicky Morgan and others are fully aware of the realities and imperatives.

Ken Coates suggested that we turn the question on its head. Rather than moulding a school and education system to the needs and requirements of modern production and employment – with its litany of inadequacies, humiliations and repressions – we should ask what modern production and employment can learn from the aspirations of progressive education. If, as Bertrand Russell suggested, we must put love at the centre of the education process should this love not find expression in the working conditions that these young people eventually find themselves subjected to? Should we not try to understand that when the economic elites of New York and elsewhere shun 'traditional education' and choose the best education that money can buy, they do so not just because they love their children but because they understand that such an education will prepare them for the demands and challenges of the world to come? Should we not recognise that each and every individual has the potential to become extraordinary, for as the engineer and poet Mike Cooley suggests;

> '*I am frequently asked if I believe that ordinary people are really able to cope with the complexities of advanced technology and modern industrial society. I have never met an ordinary person. All the people I meet are extraordinary*'.[21]

The government has offered its answer to the question of what type of schools we need. In so doing, they have generated an unprecedented crisis and our first job is to make them accountable for it. Our second job is to reject the premise of the question they sought to answer. Our third job is to fight for a vision and structure of education and society more generally where the 'extraordinary' in each of us can be unleashed.

Notes:

1. Russell, Bertrand (2010), *On Education*, Routledge. Page 201.
2. Guardian Website (2015), 'Five top reasons people become teachers - and why they quit', accessed at http://www.theguardian.com/teacher-network/2015/jan/27/five-top-reasons-teachers-join-and-quit on 02/06/16.
3. BBC News Website (2016), 'Devon school children 'damaged by education chaos'', accessed at http://www.bbc.co.uk/news/uk-england-devon-36417101 on 01/06/2016.
4. Open letter accessed at http://schoolsweek.co.uk/wp-content/uploads/2016/06/Letter-to-the-Ministers.pdf on 01/06/16.
5. See https://www.change.org/p/nicky-morgan-mp-nicky-morgan-has-failed-our-kids-she-should-resign-4fd80ad2-28d7-4f81-89f0-44c8ce7e5e3d?recruiter=46009547&utm_source=share_for_starters&utm_medium=copyLink, accessed 10/07/16.
6. Ibid.
7. See https://letthekidsbekids.wordpress.com, accessed 10/07/16.
8. See https://letthekidsbekids.wordpress.com/what-you-can-do/, accessed 10/07/16.
9. Daily Telegraph Website (2016), 'Kid's strike: Councils warn parents could be fined for taking children out of school', accessed at http://www.telegraph.co.uk/education/2016/05/03/kids-strike-thousands-of-parents-expected-to-take-children-out-o/ on 10/07/16.
10. The operation of 'covert' selection by certain secondary schools in Nottingham was a widely recognised phenomenon amongst some primary school head teachers and parents. There is no hard evidence for this practice other than plentiful anecdotes. One example of such a process is as follows: asking parents/carers to pick up application forms for the school at a set time, on a set day – a Saturday morning – thus enabling the school to identify those children with the most clued-up and/or 'aspirational' parents/carers. Other similar exercises in social

profiling were employed.

11. BBC News Website (2010), 'Schools are promised an academies 'revolution'', accessed at http://www.bbc.co.uk/news/10159448 on 10/07/16.

12. Nottingham Post Website (2013), 'Teachers' fury over Ofsted blitz on Nottingham's 'substandard' schools', accessed at http://www.nottinghampost.com/teachers-fury-ofsted-blitz-city-s-substandard/story-20244031-detail/story.html on 01/06/16.

13. Mail Online Website (2013), 'Nottingham: city where several schools are failing after inspections by Ofsted', accessed at http://www.dailymail.co.uk/news/article-2515991/Nottingham-city-schools-failing-inspections-Ofsted.html on 01/06/16.

14. Weaver, Anthony (1962) 'Jug, Clay or Flower?' in *Anarchy 21* (vol 2, no 11), quoted from Ward, Colin (1995), 'Education for Resourcefulness' in *Talking Schools*, Freedom Press.

15. Erickson, Megan (2016), 'Imagining Socialist Education' in Leonard, Sarah and Sunkara, Bhashkar eds (2016), *The Future We Want: Radical Ideas for the New Century*, Metropolitan Books.

16. Ibid.

17. Ibid.

18. Coates, Ken (1973), 'Education as a lifelong experience' in Buckman, Peter, Ed (1973), *Education Without Schools*, Souvenir Press.

19. Ibid.

20. Ibid.

21. Cooley, Mike (2016), *Architect or Bee? The Human Price of Technology*, Spokesman Books.

Contributors

Christine Blower served as the General Secretary of the National Union of Teachers between 2008 and 2016. She is now International Secretary.

Siobhan Collingwood is the head teacher of a primary school in Morcombe, Lancashire.

Mary Compton served as President of the National Union of Teachers between 2013 and 2014. Mary runs the website www.teachersolidarity.com.

Jeremy Corbyn is the Leader of the Labour Party.

Kevin Courtney is the General Secretary of the National Union of Teachers.

Alan Gibbons is the renowned author of children's books, a former teacher and campaigner for education.

Rosie Hancock is a primary school teacher.

Jill Huish is the mother of two young children and a local campaigner from Banbury, Oxfordshire.

Julie James has been a teacher for 31 years.

Sam Keely is currently studying history of the University of Liverpool.

Gawain Little is a primary school teacher in Oxford and a member of NUT's National Executive Committee.

Kristine Mayle is the Treasurer of the Chicago Teachers Union.

Philip Moriarty is Professor of Physics at the University of Nottingham.

Louise Regan is the Senior Vice President of the National Union of Teachers.

Tony Simpson edits *The Spokesman*, journal of the Bertrand Russell Peace Foundation.

Kiri Tunks is the Junior Vice President of the National Union of Teachers.

Tom Unterrainer teaches mathematics.

Nadia Whittome is a student in Nottingham.